B.

London you've seen
&
London you haven't seen!

love, J
1993

LONDON PARKS
AND GARDENS

LONDON PARKS AND GARDENS

Text by
MARIANNE BRACE

With photographs by
ERNEST FRANKL

THE PEVENSEY PRESS
Cambridge England

Front cover Hampton Court from its park

Frontispiece The parterre outside the Palm House, Kew Gardens. In the foreground is one of the Queen's Beasts, a series of ten heraldic animals; these are stone replicas of plaster originals carved by James Woodford to decorate Westminster Abbey for the Queen's coronation in 1953. They imitate a set made for Henry VIII. In the distance is the 'campanile' – in fact a disguised flue for the boiler heating the Palm House. It was designed by Decimus Burton in 1847

Back cover Buckingham Palace through the trees of Green Park

Published by The Pevensey Press
6 De Freville Avenue, Cambridge CB4 1HR, UK

Photographs: Ernest Frankl; 67–70 by permission of Syon Park

Maps: Carmen Frankl

The author gives special thanks for their help to: Simon Passmore, Rosemary Nicholson, The Chelsea Physic Garden, London Borough of Hounslow, The Wimbledon Society; and acknowledges the assistance of: The Department of the Environment; Friends of Holland Park; Friends of Gunnersbury Park & Museum; The National Trust; The Victoria & Albert Museum; Historic Buildings Division of the GLC; Royal Hospital, Chelsea; Royal Botanic Gardens, Kew; London Borough of Lambeth; The Streatham Society; The Crystal Palace Foundation

Edited by Michael Hall and Julia Harding

Designed by Jim Reader
Design and production in association with
Book Production Consultants, Cambridge

ISBN 0 907115 30 6

Typesetting in Baskerville by Westholme Graphics

Printed in Singapore

Contents

Green London   8

The Royal Parks
  Greenwich   11
  St James's Park   18
  Green Park   22
  Hyde Park   24
  Kensington Gardens and Kensington
  Palace Gardens   29
  Regent's Park and Primrose Hill   37
  Richmond Park   43
  Hampton Court and Bushy Park   50

Working Gardens
  The Royal Botanic Gardens, Kew   59
  Chelsea Physic Garden and the Royal
  Hospital Gardens, Chelsea   69
  Tradescant Garden   72

Gardens for the Gardenless
  Cannizaro Park   75
  Chiswick House   77
  Gunnersbury Park   81
  Ham House   83
  The Hill Gardens and Golders Hill Park   85
  Holland Park   86
  Kenwood and Hampstead Heath   88
  Marble Hill, Orleans House and York House   93
  Osterley Park   96
  The Rookery and Crystal Palace   98
  Syon Park   102
  Waterlow Park   107

Seasonal Guide   111

Maps
  London Parks and Gardens   6
  Greenwich Park   12
  Hampton Court and Bushy Park   52
  Royal Botanic Gardens, Kew   60
  Chiswick House Gardens   76

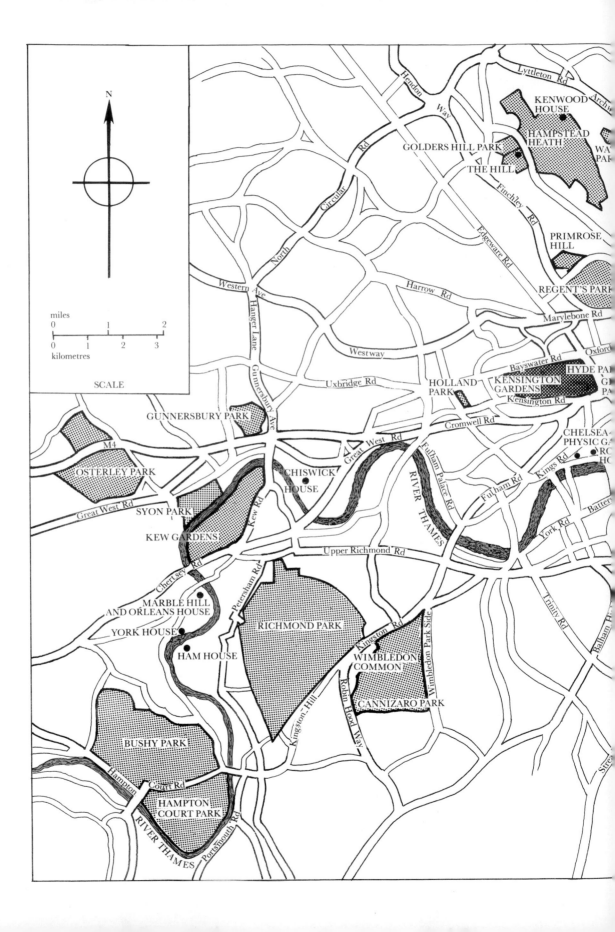

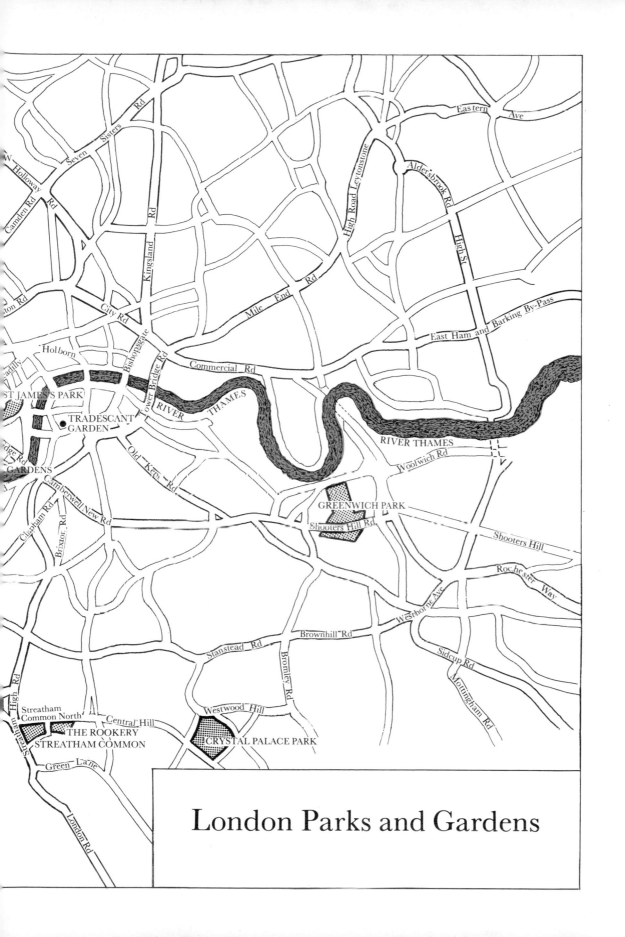

London Parks and Gardens

Green London

'. . . a pastoral landscape under the smoky sky' (Henry James, *English Hours*, 1905).

Look at any map of London. The city is flush with parks, gardens and open spaces. For people living here, parks offer a break from urban surroundings, a place to enjoy the pleasures of the country without leaving town. For visitors they are as much a part of the capital as Beefeaters and double-decker buses. No trip to London is complete without a glimpse of the Albert Memorial towering above Kensington Gardens (**20**) or a tour of the magnificent glasshouses at Kew (**46, 47**).

London has three kinds of parks and gardens. The royal parks (ten in all) belong to the Crown and are administered by the Department of the Environment. The oldest have evolved from hunting grounds and private lands attached to royal residences. They stretch in an arc from Greenwich in the south-east across central London to Hampton Court in the south-west. Then there are the gardens of historic houses, once country estates of the nobility, but now swallowed up by London. Properties like Osterley and Kenwood have survived their affluent owners, and as no individual can afford their upkeep, they are run by public authorities or charities, and their grounds are thrown open as 'gardens for the gardenless'. Finally, there are specialist gardens, or 'working gardens', such as the Chelsea Physic Garden, which welcome the public but only on certain days and at certain times. Some charge an entrance fee.

What these many parks and gardens share is greenness, which they owe to English weather, and acres of grass on which, surprisingly, you *are* allowed to walk. But it is not just their verdure which makes them worth visiting; their historical associations tell of a much older England. Who does not feel a morbid thrill in St James's, knowingly treading the same ground as Charles I on his way to the scaffold; or smile at the image of Elizabeth I holding court under a still-standing oak tree (**7**) in Greenwich?

This guide includes all those parks and gardens of special interest to visitors. Each has an individual character – you may favour the wild expanse of Richmond Park, or prefer instead civilised Green Park with its joggers and lunching office workers. The parks are never out of season and can be enjoyed in all weathers. Do not be put off by drizzle. On a wet May day, wooded areas seem more woody and flowers take on a brilliance and intensity which are less apparent in a sunnier light. There is always something to do: as well as exhibitions, outdoor concerts and plays, the parks offer swimming, rowing and horse-riding.

1 *This view of woodland at Kenwood suggests the depth of the countryside, yet Trafalgar Square is only five miles away.*

The face of London seems to alter at an alarming rate, but despite greedy redevelopers and thoughtless planners its precious green areas have been zealously preserved. They have a timelessness which defies the hectic pace around them: spend an afternoon taking tea in the walled garden at Ham (**57**) or sauntering among the avenues in Greenwich and you will discover it for yourself.

The Royal Parks

Greenwich

'The most delightful spot of ground in Great Britain', wrote Daniel Defoe when passing through Greenwich in the early 18th century. In those days it was an important river port, and its majestic buildings show what a fashionable place it came to be as a result of its reputation for clean air.

This is the oldest of the royal parks. Its 185 acres were enclosed in the 15th century but its avenues of trees, network of paths and fringe of distinguished buildings owe more to the Stuarts than to the Plantagenets responsible for its enclosure. Height and the river made Greenwich an ideal spot for invaders and settlers. The Saxons called it Grenawic, the green village, and the town is first recorded in AD 914 when Elstrudis, King Alfred's daughter, presented it to the abbots of St Peter of Ghent. The monks built a court-house overlooking the Thames where the Royal Naval College now stands. In 1414 Henry V ruled that no foreign monasteries should possess English property and confiscated the land. When he died, Humphrey, Duke of Gloucester – his brother and acting Regent – built himself a riverside manor, the Bella Vista (later renamed the Placentia), on the same plot. To protect his estate Humphrey surrounded 200 acres with wooden palings.

Many sovereigns have lived here, including Henry VIII and his three children. His court must have been a sparkling one, for this turbulent man loved entertainment: opposite the Queen's House there was tilting, archery and sword-fighting. Elizabeth I's mother, Anne Boleyn, was arrested at Greenwich, yet the palace was still Elizabeth's favourite home and it was here, according to tradition, that Sir Walter Ralegh flung down his cloak for her to walk upon.

James I built a wall around the parkland and, some say, planted the first English Mulberry trees in the grounds. His wife, meanwhile, was planning a new residence – the 'House of Delight' – and commissioned the architect Inigo Jones to design it. She died before it was finished, so it was left to Charles I to complete it for *his* wife, Henrietta Maria. Today the Queen's House forms the central part of the National Maritime Museum (**8**) and is equipped with 19th-century wings and a colonnade linking the various buildings. Its Palladian style supposedly inspired the White House in Washington D.C.

During the Commonwealth, Duke Humphrey's riverside palace fell into disrepair, and when Charles II returned from exile he demolished it. But first he attended to the grounds. While in France he had admired the formal gardens of Louis XIV, designed by André Le Nôtre. This Frenchman's talent lay in combining the features of Italian gardens (ascending terraces) with those of

2 *The Old Royal Observatory (1675), which towers over Greenwich Park, was founded by Charles II to promote scientific knowledge and to improve navigation. He also donated £500 towards the cost of construction, from the sale of spoiled gunpowder. The architect was Christopher Wren and the building incorporates wood, iron and lead from a medieval castle which once stood on this site. In 1894 a young French anarchist, Martial Bourdin, was maimed by one of his own bombs, intended for the Observatory, on a path nearby – an incident which became the basis of Conrad's novel* The Secret Agent.

11

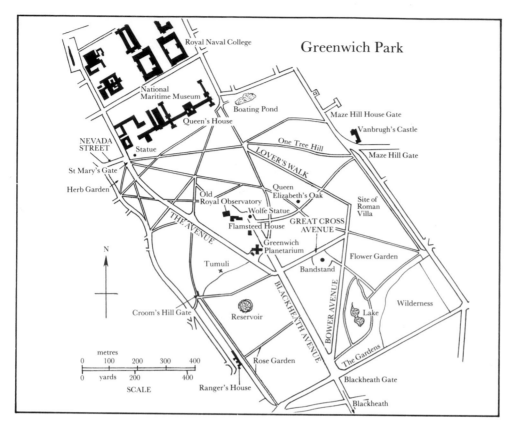

Greenwich Park

Dutch gardens (canals and avenues). Charles invited him to England, but although Le Nôtre's plans for the park were adopted it seems he never set foot in Greenwich.

In 1664 over 500 elms were planted, together with coppices, orchards and a wilderness, and Charles invited John Webb to design a palace, the King's House: a three-sided court on the river. Five years later, Charles's funds and interest had both dwindled, so work stopped, leaving the palace incomplete for twenty years. By 1675 a second project was occupying the King. Concerned to improve navigation at sea, Charles founded the Royal Observatory on the hill (**2**), the oldest surviving scientific institution in Great Britain. Here John Flamsteed, the first Astronomer Royal, developed the system of latitude and longitude. His house, designed by Sir Christopher Wren, possesses an eight-sided room intended to hold huge clocks with 13-foot pendulums for measuring Mean Time, the basis from which the world's time zones are calculated. It is now annexed to the National Maritime Museum.

In 1948 smog exiled the Royal Observatory to Herstmonceux in Sussex where the air was cleaner, but the zero meridian line of longitude still passes through Flamsteed House, marked out by a metal strip set into the cobbled ground (**4**). Stand astride it and you have one foot in the eastern and one in the western hemispheres. A 24-hour clock (**5**) on an outside wall – one of the earliest to be electrically driven – shows Greenwich Mean Time. On the roof of Flamsteed House, a time ball, visible for miles, is raised half way up a mast at five minutes to the hour and to the top at two minutes before. It drops precisely on the hour.

3 *This magnificent chestnut tree in Greenwich Park is probably one of those planted in the early 1660s for Charles II, when the park was laid out in its present form.*

King William of Orange and Queen Mary preferred the seclusion of Kensington to the grandeur of Greenwich, and so in 1694 they had the unfinished Greenwich Palace converted into a naval hospital. In 1873 it was taken over by the Royal Naval College. The public was freely admitted to the park for the first time during the early 19th century, in William IV's reign. His statue stands at St Mary's Gate. At that time the park was the setting of the annual Greenwich Fair, an occasion so riotous it was finally banned in 1870. In *Sketches by Boz* Charles Dickens wrote: 'If the parks be the lungs of London we wonder what Greenwich Fair is . . . a periodical breaking out we suppose, a sort of spring rash . . . a three days' fever which cools the blood for six months afterwards . . .'

Today the park is a more sober place. You are unlikely to meet poets 'squeaking their penny dittos', in Dickens's phrase, unless like Dr Johnson they find inspiration here. Start your tour at St Mary's Gate, Nevada Street (see map). The scented herb garden is on your right, the neat lawns and herbaceous beds of the Maritime Museum on your left. Climb the hill by way of The Avenue, taking care because it is a main road. Half way up on the right appears

Henry Moore's *Standing Figure: Knife Edge*. Just beyond it are the tumuli, virtually level with Croom's Hill Gate. There are about twenty of these saucer-shaped mounds, and many others have been destroyed by tree-planting. When in 1784 several were opened, human hair, scraps of woollen cloth and glass beads were discovered. They may be tombs dating from 1011, when the Danes camped on Blackheath, or the graves of soldiers killed in a 15th-century battle. Greenwich is riddled with underground tunnels, some of which have paved floors and are sufficiently roomy for two people to walk abreast. Possibly they supplied water to Humphrey's Bella Vista. (They are closed to the public.)

Keeping to the edge of the park, you come to the Ranger's House, a partly 17th-century building which houses the Suffolk Collection of Tudor portraits (access from the street). Opposite, the Red Dandys and Living Fires of the rose garden provide a splash of colour in June. There is also a rare Chestnut-Leaved Oak (*Quercus castaneifolia*).

Further along, by the wall, you will notice a ring of flagstones in the grass marking the site of Queen Caroline's Bath. This was hidden until 1890 when a dilapidated summer-house was demolished to expose a sunken rectangular bath with white-tiled steps leading into it. It belonged to Montagu House (demolished 1815), where once George IV's wife had lived.

Pause at Blackheath Gate to appreciate Le Nôtre's grand central avenue of chestnuts with the statue of General Wolfe (a gift from Canada in 1930) at the climax. Wolfe left his Greenwich home for Quebec to win Canada from the French in 1759. This avenue intersects with other tree-lined walks. Where Great Cross almost meets Bower Avenue grows a Prickly Castor Oil Tree.

4, 5 *(Left) The Meridian Line, outside the Old Royal Observatory, Greenwich. This narrow metal strip divides the eastern and western hemispheres. (Right) The Observatory's 24-hour clock shows Greenwich Mean Time, the basis from which the international time-zone system is calculated. The original clock was replaced in 1893 by this, one of the first electrically driven public clocks.*

6 *The tea-clipper* Cutty Sark, *one of the last merchant sailing ships, was built at Dumbarton on the Clyde in 1869. Now an education centre for the merchant navy and a museum, it has been moored at Greenwich since 1954.*

8 *The National Maritime Museum, with the Royal Naval College in the distance, seen from the Old Royal Observatory. The white building in the centre is the Queen's House (1616–35), by Inigo Jones. The paths laid out by Le Nôtre can be seen criss-crossing the wide expanse of the park.*

Greenwich is famous for its rare trees. In the enclosed area east of Blackheath Gate you will find cedars, Indian Bean and Paper Birch trees and a Pride of India introduced from the Orient in 1763. As you enter The Gardens here, you are greeted by a vast Sweet Chestnut, which dates from the early 1660s and is therefore one of Charles II's original saplings. The garden has large circular beds and a sinuous lake with armies of ducks and swans. Grey squirrels are numerous, too, and tame – they have been known to demand food by running up the legs of surprised tourists. Also in this corner is the 13-acre Wilderness, a fenced-in sanctuary for the fallow deer which have graced the park since the 16th century or earlier. At the turn of the century Henry James described them as being 'as tame as sleepy children'. But they were also rather mischievous, helping themselves to people's biscuits and indulging tastes for unusual foods. One died from eating too much gooseberry tart, another from following a diet of orange peel – an autopsy revealed two hatfuls in its stomach.

Leave the herbaceous beds and join Bower Avenue, where a sign points to Queen Elizabeth's Oak (**7**). Planted in the 12th century, this tree died more than a hundred years ago but still stands entangled in creepers and ivy. Anne Boleyn and Henry VIII danced beneath it; their daughter Elizabeth I took refreshments inside the hollow. A door and window were made in its bark, and park offenders have been locked inside as punishment. East of the oak is the site of a Roman villa, also protected by railings. All that remains is fragments of mosaic floor, though the original excavations unearthed coins and tiles.

7 *Queen Elizabeth's Oak, a giant tree which was hollowed out to make a lock-up for park offenders. Henry VIII and Ann Boleyn are said to have danced around it and Elizabeth I occasionally took refreshments inside. It died c. 1880.*

Before descending the steep Lover's Walk, you might make a last sortie up the now oddly named One Tree Hill to admire the view from the top, or nip through Maze Hill Gate on the east to gape at England's first folly: Vanbrugh's castle of 1719. And do explore Blackheath, south of the park – the rallying point in 1381 for the Peasant's Revolt against poll taxes and corrupt officials.

St James's Park

'I go to walk in the park which is now everyday more and more pleasant' (Samuel Pepys, 1662). If you consider Nelson's Column to stand at the very heart of London, then St James's Park is the capital's most central green space. Its 93 acres form a civilised oasis in the midst of the frenetic West End and have been the backdrop to four centuries of pomp and circumstance. The northern boundary is The Mall, running from Admiralty Arch (commemorating Edward VII) to Buckingham Palace. Marking the way are Carlton House Terrace and three mansions, Marlborough, Clarence and Lancaster, like ladies-in-waiting attending the palace itself. Sixteenth-century St James's Palace, still the Court's official residence, is also situated here. To the east loom the curiously exotic spires and cupolas of Government buildings in Whitehall. The Admiralty and the Treasury flank Horse Guards Parade, which has an 18th-century clocktower. The Changing of the Guard takes place here daily, and in June this is where the Queen inspects the Trooping of the Colour. Just to the south, obscured by other buildings, soar the Houses of Parliament and Westminster Abbey. Wherever you turn there is magnitude and power.

St James's vies with Greenwich for the distinction of being the first royal park. Although Greenwich was emparked earlier it became royal later. St James's was acquired in 1532 to swell the private lands of the King. Once a marshy district, good only for grazing hogs, it surrounded a hospital for leprous maidens, founded by the citizens of London and dedicated to St James. In the 13th century a fair was held here, beginning on the eve of the saint's day and lasting for the next five. The city's shops stayed closed and the profits of the fair were donated to the maidens. In the 16th century, however, Henry VIII turned his greedy eye on the land. He struck a deal with the hospital's trustees and threw out the fourteen inmates (appeasing his conscience by providing them with pensions). St James's Palace replaced the hospital, of which today only the gatehouse survives.

Henry drained the parkland, walled it off and introduced herds of deer. He also set up a tilt-yard, for tournaments, on the site of Horse Guards Parade. James I enclosed another 4 acres, where Buckingham Palace now stands, and cultivated Mulberry trees for the manufacture of silk. (Now only one Mulberry grows in the park, opposite Queen Anne's Gate.) During the Commonwealth this spot became *the* place to eat cheesecake, syllabub and mulberry tarts *al fresco*.

James also established a private zoo in the park, stocked with gifts from foreign kings. Keepers costumed in red and gold looked after leopards, camels, even a crocodile or two. There was also an elephant, which was treated to a gallon of wine a day. St James's was closed after the execution of Charles I and many of its trees were felled by Parliament for fuel. When Charles II returned to London he found his grounds depleted, but even so he opened them to the public in the autumn of 1660. Charles intended to turn the rural acres into attractive pleasure gardens. He invited the assistance of Le Nôtre, the French landscape designer who planned Greenwich Park, but the Frenchman declined, saying he would not ruin the park's rustic charm. The King was undeterred. To the north The Mall was laid out. Like its neighbour Pall Mall, it takes its name from the French game *paille maille*, a form of croquet. The Mall was paved with crushed cockleshells and lined with double rows of trees. These days no one

9 *Buckingham Palace from St James's Park. On the right is the Queen Victoria Memorial; the Queen is shown in white marble on the base, below a gilded figure of Victory. The main façade of the palace was rebuilt in 1913.*

plays *paille maille* on what has since become a busy thoroughfare, but you might see lunching office workers indulging in a little Mediterranean boule near the Queen Victoria Memorial Gardens.

Birdcage Walk was formed along the southern boundary, its rows of trees on either side decked with the cages of parrots and small fowl. A keen ornithologist, Charles II had a canal created with a Duck Island, complete with decoy and crowds of birds from the Thames Marshes. Other plumed and decorative species made this their haunt too. The actress Nell Gwyn owned a house just outside and – according to the diarist John Evelyn – would lean over her garden wall and call to her lover the King in the park.

In harsh winters like that of 1662 people skated on the canal – a Dutch pastime introduced by the Cavaliers. In summer, visitors would enjoy the mild weather, snoozing or singing songs with friends beneath the trees. The King liked strolling here alone – so much so that his unpopular Catholic brother James warned him against it. Charles, however, retorted: 'But who would kill *me* to make *you* King?' Drawing your sword in St James's was an offence, and it was the one place in town where no arrest could be made. Only the Board of Green Cloth, part of the Lord Steward's Office, had jurisdiction over the area. In 1677 they sent the unfortunate Richard Harris to Bedlam (the lunatic asylum) for hurling an orange at the King here. After Charles's death the park's fortunes declined. Under Queen Anne it became notorious for whores, and although the gates were locked at night nearly 6,500 people had access to keys. During the reigns of George I and George II, St James's was the place for wagers. Fat men raced old men; an 18-month-old girl crawled the length of The

10 *Not Leningrad but London: St James's Park in winter, with Whitehall in the distance (the pinnacles belong to Whitehall Court, a block of flats by Archer & Green, 1884). Although the lake stilll freezes over from time to time, skating is rare because of the rule that the ice must be 4 inches thick.*

Mall in thirty minutes; a calico printer achieved fame by winning hopping matches. Duelling was rife, and it became unsafe to venture out alone in case you were set upon by Mohocks, a group of gallants styling themselves on savage Indians.

By the 19th century the smart set had deserted St James's, and the park never regained its fashionable reputation. But before this happened, in 1814, it saw the anniversary of the Hanoverian succession celebrated in style. The architect John Nash designed a Chinese bridge straddling the canal on which fireworks were lit. Unfortunately it proved unsound and burst into flames, killing two spectators. Nevertheless Nash was commissioned to improve the park. He tried to rid it of its rigid French formality by turning the canal into a sinuous lake with an island at each end – the lower one called Duck Island after its predecessor. He designed the imposing Carlton House Terrace, and transformed Buckingham House into a palace.

The Mall comes to a climax with Thomas Brock's 82-foot-high memorial to Queen Victoria opposite Buckingham Palace, where a flag flies at full mast when the Queen is in residence. Cross the road to enter the park on the south side of The Mall and follow the lake to the bridge, which dates from 1957. From the middle you have one of the loveliest views in London. To the west are the palace, the memorial and a row of Swamp Cypresses and Weeping Willows dipping into the water (**9**). To the east the turrets of Whitehall are glimpsed behind chandelier-like fountains (**10**), installed to aerate the water after 3,000 fish floated to the surface in 1960, dead from lack of oxygen. Forty species of

11 *Pelicans and Canada Geese on and around Duck Island, St James's Park. Pelicans were introduced into the park in the 17th century, a gift from the Russian ambassador. They are large, long-living (some reach sixty years of age) and aggressively greedy – they have been known to swallow up live pigeons.*

waterfowl – 900 birds in total – live on or around the lake (**11**). There are pelicans too, in residence since the 17th century – a gift to Charles II from the Russian ambassador. As well as the more usual duck life, watch out for pigeons and gulls who swoop with a predatory glint in their eye at anyone so foolish as to be holding bread. During summer lunchtimes strains of music hover in the air as military bands strike up on the bandstand (**13**), and the area becomes a sea of green deckchairs with people savouring the performance.

Green Park

'I have a weakness for the convenient, familiar, treeless, or almost treeless, expanse of the Green Park, and the friendly part it plays as a kind of encouragement to Piccadilly', wrote Henry James in *English Hours* (1905). What a pleasant surprise he would have today. It is one of the pleasures of a stroll in this area to stand with your back to Buckingham Palace and stare up Green Park's Broad Walk towards Piccadilly, now seen through an aisle of graciously arching branches.

No park is so aptly named as this. Limes, planes and hawthorns line intersecting paths furnished with old-fashioned street lamps and benches. English gardeners take their lawns seriously, and this particular park has more than most. Apart from a sprinkling of spring bulbs hemming the Queen's Walk and Constitution Hill there are few flowers, and it feels surprisingly urban; it is hard to believe that sheep grazed here as late as 1948.

12 *The Queen Mother's Rose Walk, St James's Park, established in 1980 as a tribute to the Queen Mother on her eightieth birthday. The varieties she chose were Korresia, Congratulations, Just Joey, Blessings, Young Venturer and Scented Air. The lake, and the bridge that crosses it, are visible in the distance to the right.*

13 *The bandstand in
St James's Park. Between
May and September the
bands of the Coldstream
Guards, the Irish Guards,
and the Blues and Royals
perform to large,
appreciative audiences.*

At its south-easterly corner Green Park meets St James's Park. The park's 53
acres were probably at one time the burial ground for the lepers of the former
hospital in St James's. Charles II was responsible for enclosing the area, then
known as Upper St James's Park. Constitution Hill is so called because of
Charles's 'democratic' behaviour in walking among his subjects there. (Queen's
Walk on the eastern edge is quite the opposite: a private path constructed for
Caroline of Ansbach, George II's queen, so that she could stroll alone.)

Unlike the neighbouring park, Upper St James's had no ban on sword-
drawing and so it became a venue for duels. It was here in 1771 that Edward,
Viscount Ligonier, fought the Italian poet Count Alfieri, who was having an
affair with his wife. Though badly wounded, Alfieri returned to the Haymarket
Theatre to watch the play's finale. He said 'Ligonier did not kill me because he
did not want to, and I did not kill him because I did not know how.'

Other displays of prowess took the form of military parades and public
celebrations. The end of the war of Austrian succession (1740–8) was welcomed
with a grand firework party. A huge Temple of Peace was erected in the park,
decked with artificial flowers and showing George II bringing peace to
Britannia. Crowning this was a burning sun. Handel composed special inci-
dental music and a hundred cannons were poised to fire in time to the beat. But
as the cannons roared and music sounded, disaster struck. The temple ignited
and set fire to a nearby building.

Through the centre of the park runs Broad Walk, designed to draw the eye to
Queen Victoria's Memorial in The Mall. The ornamental Dominion Gates,
presented by the British Dominions, are matched at the northern end by the
Devonshire Gates, which have decorative stags and sphinxes. Dating from the
18th century, they once belonged to the Duke of Devonshire's Chiswick home

(see pp. 77–81) but were moved to Devonshire House, Piccadilly (now demolished). During World War I someone suggested melting them down for ammunition. Despite their reprieve they seem a little sad, leading nowhere, their motto 'Cavendo tutus' (Safe in Watchfulness) made redundant – except with reference to the traffic just outside.

Hyde Park

'There could be nothing less like London . . . and yet it takes London, of all cities, to give you such an impression of the country' (Henry James, *English Hours*, 1905). On a fine summer's day, as many as 100,000 people may visit Hyde Park. The 360 acres are only a few minutes from Oxford Street in one direction and Knightsbridge in another, and rising above its trees are Park Lane's grand hotels: Grosvenor House, the Dorchester and, tallest of all, the Hilton. You may witness the Household Cavalry on parade, or catch a veteran-car rally. And it is not just children and dogs who run about here, according to the Park Keeper who once met a young woman exercising her pet leopard.

Park Lane was once part of Watling Street, and Oxford Street was the Via Trinobantina, so Hyde Park is bounded at the east and north by Roman roads. In Saxon times it formed part of the Manor of Eia, which fell into the hands of Geoffrey de Mandeville after the Norman Conquest. The estate was subdivided and one third, the Manor of Hyde, was given to the monks of Westminster Abbey, who farmed the land and prayed for Geoffrey's soul. All went well until 1536, when Henry VIII wanted to extend his hunting grounds and annexed the estate. It remained a private enclosure until the 17th century, when Charles I

14 *A distant view of Buckingham Palace through the trees of Green Park. Today the freedom to walk over the grass is taken for granted but it is thanks to the 19th-century Prime Minister Lord Palmerston that an attempt to keep visitors to the paths was scotched: the grass, he said, was to be 'walked upon freely and without restraint by the people old and young, for whose enjoyment the parks are maintained'.*

opened it to his subjects. At this time the celebrated 'Ring' was laid out, a circular carriage track where anyone who was anyone had to be seen doing the circuit. During the Restoration a Keeper was on hand to spread water on the dust raised by the horses, and nearby a cheesecake house offered refreshment. (To the east lay Daisy Walk, another spot where the privileged used to go round in circles: here in the early 20th century an army of nannies could be seen pushing the baby-carriages of the Upper Classes.)

Even during the Interregnum the park stayed modish, much to the annoyance of the Puritans, who insisted that it should close on Sundays. Oliver Cromwell took the air here, and one day was almost killed when he fell from his carriage and was dragged along behind it; to make matters worse a loaded pistol went off in his pocket. In 1652 he sold the park in three lots to buyers who found, to their chagrin, that the sales were not recognised after the Restoration.

Charles II restocked the park with game and circled it with a wall. During the plague of 1665 it was peopled by camping soldiers and refugees from infected areas. But only three years later society returned, flouncing in its finery, flirting with orange-sellers and doing the 'tour' of The Ring. Under Queen Anne rowdier elements were partially controlled by restricting the entry of certain vehicles and forbidding the Park Keepers to sell liquor. Even so, robberies became commonplace, and well into the 18th century it was dangerous to walk alone here at night. King William III, having chosen Kensington as his home, had 300 oil lamps hung along the southern carriage drive, making it one of the first public highways in England to be artificially lit. He also appointed guards

15 Achilles *in Hyde Park, unveiled in 1822, was designed by Sir Richard Westmacott as a tribute to the Duke of Wellington, who lived nearby in Apsley House. The choice of a nude male figure for a monument paid for by the women of England attracted much criticism at the time. The reaction of the Duke of Wellington is not known.*

to patrol the grounds at night. When a footpad was caught he was dispatched without delay to the north-east corner of the park, where he was hanged from Tyburn-tree. Eight men could swing on each side of these gallows, which provided a gruesome spectator sport until 1759. When the notorious highwayman Jack Sheppard had his 'neck stretched' he attracted 200,000 people, many of whom must have been hoping he would devise another daring escape. As soon as smart houses were built in the area, the gallows were moved to Newgate and this corner was renamed Cumberland Gate.

Henry VIII's original parkland forfeited about 300 acres when in 1730 George II's wife, Caroline of Ansbach, commanded the architect and landscape designer William Kent to create a lake deep and broad enough to hold two yachts. This he did by turning six connecting pools into the winding Serpentine. In the course of dredging, great tree trunks surfaced; they had been used by the Westminster monks to shore up the sides of their fish-ponds. The King, mistakenly believing his wife was paying with her own money rather than with public funds, also improved the carriage road between Kensington and St James's. Running along the southern perimeter, the 'Route du Roi' is now known as Rotten Row or The Mile. Since the last century this tree-lined stretch has been *the* place to ride, and there were cries of protest when in the 1960s someone suggested turning it into a running track.

The park has been the location for many festive events. In 1814 it was turned into a temporary fairground to celebrate (prematurely) Napoleon's defeat, in 1856 the end of the Crimean War was marked by a firework display and in 1981 the marriage of Prince Charles to Lady Diana Spencer saw the skies above the park illuminated by two and half tons of explosives. Because of its central

16 *On a summer's day Hyde Park is full of people relaxing and enjoying themselves, but the sense of a great open space is never lost.*

17 *Deckchairs beside the north shore of the Serpentine in Hyde Park. This 40-acre lake, created for Queen Caroline by William Kent in 1730, was made large enough to hold two royal yachts. Rowing boats have been available for hire here since 1847.*

18 *Speakers' Corner, Hyde Park. As long as you avoid obscenity and sedition and don't ask for money, you can say anything here—and people do, both on the platforms and in the audience.*

position, Hyde Park was selected to house the Great Exhibition of 1851. Approximately 18 acres accommodated Joseph Paxton's glass hall, which covered an area three times the size of St Paul's Cathedral. There were 13,937 exhibitors and 6,039,195 visitors, including an 85-year-old Cornish woman who walked to London from her home in Penzance. It took her five weeks, and she made the 300-mile return journey on foot as well. The exhibition hall was subsequently moved to Sydenham, where it remained until fire destroyed it in 1936. The ornate Coalbrookdale Gates on the south carriage road, east of the Albert Memorial, are the only reminders: they were one of the exhibits in 1851.

Begin your walk at Apsley Gate, Hyde Park Corner. Apsley House, now a museum, was the Duke of Wellington's home. To the left, the Triple Archway (*c.*1828), by Decimus Burton, carries reliefs copied from the Parthenon frieze. Beyond the gate glowers Sir Richard Westmacott's *Achilles* (**15**), sometimes called 'The Ladies' Trophy'. A committee of ladies raised the £10,000 needed to forge this tribute to Wellington. Cast in bronze from French guns taken at Wellington's victories, he is so mammoth that part of the park wall had to come down in order to get him in. To the north-west grows a very rare Yellow Wood Tree (*Cladastris lutea*), which has smooth, grey bark and leaves that turn bright yellow in autumn.

Following Broad Walk to the end you arrive at the possible site of the Tyburn Gallows, or Tyburn-tree, indicated by a stone, and Nash's Marble Arch (1828), originally a gateway to Buckingham Palace and moved here in 1851. But before that, stop at Speakers' Corner (**18**), where every Sunday afternoon you can witness one of England's great institutions. Forum for free speech, soap-box venue, licence for lunatics, call it what you will, it is always amusing and attracts crowds of mostly good-natured hecklers. The speakers may range from the odd stand-up comic to dour women in cagoules demanding Sapphic rights. The corner's origins date back to 1866 when the Reform League, mobilising support for universal male suffrage, wished to hold a mass rally in the park, to the consternation of the Commissioner of Police. (What would he have said to the pop concerts and CND rallies which have taken place since?) Permission refused, the demonstrators besieged the park, tearing down railings and fighting with police. In 1872 the situation was reviewed and this meeting point designated for people to speak their minds.

Return to the north shore of the Serpentine (**17**), which in summer resembles a seaside front with its deckchairs, roller-skaters and excitable children. The lake itself changes with the seasons. In winter it can be opaque, even forbidding: in December 1816 Harriet Westbrook, Shelley's first wife, pregnant and deserted, drowned herself here. But winter has its advantages: in 1825 a Mr Hunt won a wager when he drove a coach-and-four across the icy surface, and in 1861 50,000 skaters whirled about and took refreshment at the many stalls lining the banks. These activities are part of the past, but you can still hire one of the rowing boats, a facility dating from 1847. Opposite the boating house a small island serves as a bird sanctuary. You may fish, providing you have a permit and return your catch to the water, alive.

East of the lake, beyond the restaurant, lies a small hollow area with flowers and a waterfall. Near this dell a Druidical stone, sometimes said to have been brought from Stonehenge, is actually part of a 19th-century drinking fountain. In spring this whole area is carpeted in crocuses and snowdrops. More horticultural interest is provided by the Wing Nut and Dove Trees on either side of

19 *Summer in Hyde Park. Even though it is in the very heart of the metropolis, the park can have an atmosphere of almost rural seclusion that is a reminder of the days when it was Henry VIII's private hunting ground.*

Ladies' Ride, just north of Albert Gate. Taking the southern path, with the Serpentine on your right, you arrive at the Lido, where between April and September you may swim. The swimming club here is said to be the oldest in England. Each Christmas Day the ice is broken so that members can take a dip.

Further along is the Rennie Bridge (1826), which marks the division between Hyde Park and Kensington Gardens.

Kensington Gardens and Kensington Palace Gardens

'We walked out to Kensington and strolled through the delightful gardens. It is a glorious thing for the King to keep such walks so near the metropolis open to all his subjects' (James Boswell, 1763). The 275 acres of Kensington Gardens have a genteel charm. No noisy cars are admitted, as they are in neighbouring Hyde Park, and the only whirr of wheels comes from prams – or from roller-skaters practising their turns and loops on Broad Walk. Children love these gardens. There are flat open stretches for flying kites in autumn; a round pond for sailing toy boats; a playground; and a kindred spirit in the statue of Peter Pan (**23**).

Princess Margaret lives in the red-brick palace (**21**) on the western edge of the gardens. Today you might glimpse a royal car but in the past rulers and ruled rubbed shoulders more freely. At the start of the 19th century, for instance, Caroline of Brunswick, the Prince Regent's wife, shocked visitors by running around hatless in the grounds and striking up conversations with complete strangers. Three-year-old Princess Victoria, however, charmed them by riding a donkey dressed in blue ribbons. Born in Kensington Palace, it was here that in 1837, at the age of eighteen, she was informed that she had become

Queen. When the asthmatic Dutch king, William III, came to England he rejected the damp Greenwich Palace in favour of Kensington House, which he bought in 1689 for 18,000 guineas. Sir Christopher Wren refurbished the building and added an extra floor, while William and Mary, both ardent gardeners, tackled the surrounding 26 acres of the palace gardens, accessible from Kensington Gardens, and now open to the public.

They promoted the Dutch style in gardens: enclosed areas with neat flower-beds and well-trimmed yew, holly and box hedges. This, of course, is not to everyone's taste and when Anne, Mary's sister, became Queen she swept away the dark evergreens and rigid layout. She wanted an *English* garden. Adding 30 acres to the existing area, she encircled it all with a ha-ha (see p. 93) and created a sunken garden on the site of a gravel pit. In 1702 Sir John Vanbrugh and Nicholas Hawksmoor designed an orangery where she could hold soirées. Today it is furnished with statuary from Windsor presented by Queen Elizabeth II.

20 *The Albert Memorial, Kensington Gardens, is the nation's chief monument to Queen Victoria's husband, who died in 1861. The architect, Sir George Gilbert Scott, described it as 'a colossal statue of the Prince, placed beneath a vast and magnificent shrine or tabernacle, and surrounded by works of sculpture illustrating those arts and sciences which he fostered'.*

21 *Kensington Palace, seen from Kensington Gardens. The late-17th-century palace is open to the public. In the foreground is Princess Louise's statue of her mother, Queen Victoria, who was born in the palace in 1819. The statue was erected in honour of the Queen's Golden Jubilee.*

Kensington Gardens owe their present style to the canny wife of George II. It was Queen Caroline who separated them from Hyde Park and with the help of her gardener, Charles Bridgeman, planted great avenues of trees which give the gardens their brooding air. In addition to a concentration of more familiar species, Kensington boasts rarities like the Yellow Oak and Montpelier Maple. The most impressive avenue, the 50-foot-wide Broad Walk, runs up from Palace Gate towards Black Lion Gate in the north. Unfortunately the original elms were felled in 1953 because of disease; limes and Norway Maples were planted in their place. The Queen's other decorative additions included the round pond, designed to be seen from the palace windows, a classical temple not far from the Albert Memorial, and the Long Water, a continuation of the Serpentine.

During George II's reign Kensington Gardens were open to visitors at weekends in the King's absence. Formal dress was compulsory; soldiers and servants were banned. Despite this, bad sorts still found a way in and the King himself was robbed while walking alone. When he asked if he could keep a worthless seal on his watch-chain his assailant said he would return the trinket at the same place the next day if the King promised to tell no one. A bargain was struck and the seal duly restored to its owner. It was only after the King's death that the incident came to light. George III, unlike his parents, had no wish to make Kensington a permanent home, and the royal apartments were closed for forty years. The public, however, gained freer access to the park, which from the 19th century stayed open all year round.

Start your visit at the Albert Memorial (**20**), by Queen's Gate, for what would Kensington Gardens be without it? This monument to Queen Victoria's consort is either admired or abhorred, but its 173 feet rival the Taj Mahal as a testament of personal devotion. When Albert died of typhoid in 1861 his widow wanted a memorial erected as near as possible to the site of the Great Exhibition, which the Prince had organised. Sir George Gilbert Scott designed the neo-Gothic shrine, worked in marble, bronze and semi-precious stones. The project took nine years and cost £120,000. It exalts both Albert and the Empire. A preliminary flight of steps leads to four groups of marble figures, one at each corner, representing the continents. Europe is symbolised by a bull, Asia by an elephant, Africa by a camel, and America by a bison. The base of the canopy carries a frieze with portraits of 169 Victorian heroes of the arts; above this are marble groups personifying industry. Allegorical figures are depicted in the mosaic tympana, while in the bronze spire loom the Christian virtues and the sciences. Amid this crowded hubbub sits the once-gilded 15-foot Prince holding a copy of the Great Exhibition catalogue and leaning forward slightly as if trying to catch faint strains of music issuing from the Royal Albert Hall opposite (built 1867–71).

Lancaster Walk runs directly north of this action-packed structure. Half way along, seven paths radiate from a bronze horse and rider, *Physical Energy* by

23 *The famous statue of Peter Pan by George Frampton in its secluded home in Kensington Gardens. Many of the squirrels and rabbits that adorn its base have been worn smooth, stroked by generations of small children.*

22 *The sunken garden in Kensington Palace gardens, designed in 1909, has an oblong pool at its centre surrounded by tubs containing Dwarf Cypresses. Flower-beds, in which roses follow the spring bulbs, ascend to shrub-covered walls and a pleached lime walk.*

G. F. Watts. Just beyond the memorial take the left-hand path into Flower Walk, laid out in 1843. On either side weave curvy flower-beds and neatly manicured lawns with a backdrop of trees, including an unusual Cork Oak and a Chinese Persimmon on the left. In the spring, tulips, hyacinths and wallflowers spread their colour, while in summer fuchsias, brilliantly clashing begonias and geraniums take over.

Broad Walk strikes off to the right, appearing to vanish over the horizon. About half way along, a bland marble statue of Victoria by her daughter Louise sits just outside the palace garden (**21**). Just inside is the sunken garden (**22**), designed in 1909 on the model of Queen Anne's, surrounded by a tunnel of pleached limes with openings which permit a peep at the tiered flower-beds and oblong pool. In summer, red roses and bedding plants succeed the predominantly yellow spring bulbs. North of the sunken garden is the baroque orangery and on the lawn beyond that a Date Plum and a rare *Euodia* tree.

The 7-acre round pond is a short distance from Broad Walk. Generations of children have thrilled to the excitement of sailing model boats on the water, and in 1970, when the pond was drained, hundreds of wrecked vessels were discovered trapped in the mud, together with the alloy sceptre from Victoria's statue, stolen four years earlier. In a thicket of trees to the north grows a very scarce True Service Tree, which has attractive pinky-orange bark. The Long Water lies ahead to the east. In a neat clearing set back from its edge lives Peter Pan, with a sentimental entourage of bunnies, squirrels and mice. The sculptor was Sir George Frampton (1912). Peter Pan's creator, J. M. Barrie, lived a few

24 *Fountains at the head of the Long Water, Kensington Gardens. They draw water from springs which for centuries were valued for medicinal purposes. The statue is of Dr Edward Jenner (by William Calder Marshall, 1858), pioneer of vaccination.*

25 *North Flower Walk, Kensington Gardens. The fuchsias provide a gorgeous display of colour throughout the summer.*

27 The Arch, a 19-foot-high sculpture by Henry Moore, stands beside the eastern shore of the Long Water in Kensington Gardens. Carved from Roman Travertine, it was unveiled in 1980.

26 The Pets' Cemetery, behind Victoria Lodge in the north-eastern corner of Kensington Gardens. The first interment was of a dog belonging to the Duchess of Cambridge (the Duke was Park Ranger); the dog had been run over outside Victoria Gate, and died in the lodge.

hundred yards away in the Bayswater Road. At the top of the lake, the Italian Gardens have ornate fountains (**24**) and a pavilion inspired by the Petit Trianon at Versailles and supposedly designed by Prince Albert. Queen Anne's Bower – a grand wooden alcove – makes a good shelter in sudden downpours.

The Pets' Cemetery (**26**) by Victoria Gate (behind the lodge) has 300 tiny graves (the plot is not open to the public). From the road you can peer over the railings and identify one or two headstones. The Duke of Cambridge started the trend for burying domestic animals here when in 1880 he said the last rites over his wife's favourite dog. The final burial was in 1915.

A 19-foot-high sculpture by Henry Moore (**27**) stands proudly on the eastern shore of the Long Water, an excellent spot for admiring the view of the gardens stretching back towards Kensington. Once you have crossed the bridge, the Serpentine Gallery can be seen on your right. Originally a tea room, it is now a venue for exhibitions. Here you can step out of the green into cool white rooms, their walls covered with the works of modern masters.

Regent's Park and Primrose Hill

'. . . will give a sort of glory to the Regent's Government which will be more felt by remote posterity than the victories of Trafalgar and Waterloo . . ' (Henry Crabb Robinson). Regent's Park is the remarkable result of some shrewd commercial thinking on the part of the Prince Regent (later George IV) and his advisors, who at the beginning of the 19th century laid out the whole area north of Marylebone Road and south of Prince Albert Road as an exclusive residential area of elegant buildings arranged in a park. Today the parkland (402 acres) falls into two concentric circles: an inner one with gardens and an outer one with terraces and other buildings. Main roads bordered by white stuccoed crescents (**29**) skirt the circumference and the park now houses a zoo, an outdoor theatre, and even an Islamic cultural centre.

Once part of the Great Middlesex Forest, which in medieval times spread north of London, the land occupied by Regent's Park belonged to the Manor of Tyburn, first recorded in 1279. By about 1400 a village had sprung up on the banks of the local river, the Ty. As its church was dedicated to St Mary, the area became known as Marylebone (St Mary by the bourn). The manor was rebuilt by a Thomas Hobson, and his family lived there until ejected by Henry VIII in 1538. The ageing King was getting corpulent and no longer wanted to cover great distances in search of game. Marylebone offered a good hunting ground near to home. In the next century, James I, finding himself short of money, sold Marylebone Manor, but retained the land for himself. Charles I, also in financial straits, especially during the Civil War, mortgaged the land for gunpowder. Like the other royal properties, it was seized by the Roundheads, who felled the trees for shipbuilding and sold the land to three buyers. When Charles II returned and took possession few of the original trees were still standing, and the parkland was a patchwork of farms and fields divided by hedges.

At the end of the 18th century John Fordyce, a Scottish civil servant, saw there was money to be made by developing the park. But although it was already served by the Marylebone highway, the district seemed remote. The architect John Nash hit on a solution. He would carve a grand processional road from the Prince's country home (to be built in the park) to Carlton House, his St James's residence. This route is now Regent's Street. Instead of creating a grid of residential squares and streets, Nash wanted to retain the spaciousness of parkland, with terraces built around it and neo-classical villas within. There were to be fifty-six of the latter, with such uninterrupted views that each occupant could imagine the generous acreage belonged to him alone. Half the land would remain free of buildings but there would be room for shops and markets too. In October 1811 Nash got the go-ahead and the land was sub-divided into plots. Tree-planting and road-laying began but speculators were slow to follow, and it was six years before work commenced on the first villa. Of the fifty-six intended properties only eight were built. The country home of the Prince never materialised; Nash went wildly over budget, quarrelled with the speculators and diverted his energies to refurbishing Buckingham Palace. Nevertheless, a walk in the Outer Circle and a study of the terraces give a good idea of what Nash wanted. Each row is distinctive, yet harmonises successfully with the others as part of a master plan.

The park became public in the 19th century. It was Prince Albert who introduced herbaceous beds into Broad Walk. This gracious avenue (**28**), running parallel to the eastern boundary, is bordered by giant granite urns that overflow with flowers in summer. Nash saw the walk as continuing the line from Regent Street and Portland Place. Some of the chestnuts that he planted have now been replaced by saplings. Chester Road cuts the walk into two unequal sections; it is the southern part which turns amateur gardeners green with envy. In summer the beds on the western edge of the walk become a riot of colourful

28 *Broad Walk, Regent's Park, in winter, a view reminiscent of one of Camille Pissarro's paintings of London. This long pedestrian walk runs from the north side of the park to the south, skirting the zoo at its northern end.*

Red-Hot Pokers, purple delphiniums and orange poppies. Few can resist this brazen display, and even yashmaked ladies can become quite skittish when faced with all that colour.

York Gate is the spot to start your walk. Cross the bridge over the southern tip of the lake and keep to the road. Immediately on your left, on the site of Nash's South Villa, is a red-brick building which housed Bedford College (part of London University) until 1985. The road leads over the Inner Circle to the stately gilded gates presented by Sigismund Goetze (1935). Behind them spread the flower-beds of Queen Mary's Gardens (**31**), named after George V's consort. A narrow path to the left leads to a restaurant and a main walk stretches ahead, culminating in a fountain. To the left of this is the entrance to the Open Air Theatre, which has been playing a summer season here since 1932. Come shine or drizzle the company performs to as many as 1,185 people a night. Shakespeare and the other classics gain from outdoor production; in *A Midsummer Night's Dream*, for example, the trees and bushes of the park become the wood where the lovers sleep and as night descends you may hear a real owl tooting eerily. Another traditional event in the Inner Circle is the London Harness Horse Parade every Easter.

Take the narrow path immediately to the right of the gates through which you entered the gardens. It leads to a small lake where a wooden bridge (sometimes closed) gives access to an island smothered in alpine plants. On the far side of the lake a waterfall cascades wantonly down a hill created with earth excavated from the main boating lake. To your right roses crowd beds circled

29 *Cornwall Terrace (1821), one of the splendid stuccoed terraces designed by John Nash which are such a memorable feature of Regent's Park.*

30 *This mosque is Regent's Park's newest landmark. The bronze dome, which will eventually weather to a green colour, is 75 feet high. It forms part of the Islamic Cultural Centre and the furnishings include floors of marble from Algeria, tiles from Turkey, carpets from Iran, and chandeliers from Jordan, demonstrating the extent of the Islamic world.*

with trellised pillars covered in climbers. Cross this rose garden and go through the gate. Cross the road and turn left for St John's Lodge, another of the eight original villas. Turn off into the drive which runs to the right of the building. The garden which appears on your right is a peaceful haven of herbaceous beds, statues, lawns and a mass of roses, disturbed only by the distant calls of zoo animals.

On leaving St John's Lodge, turn right and follow the road to The Holme, a villa designed *c.* 1818 by the 18-year-old Decimus Burton for his father. Nash was so impressed that he offered the young man a professional training. For the first time in this tour the extent of the park becomes visible, in the open vistas to the left. Take the next turning on the left and walk towards the bandstand between The Holme and the back of the old Bedford College building. Music from military bands fills the air at lunchtimes and early evenings from May to September. The waters of the main lake extend just behind; both the lake and the six small islands it contains were artificially made. Follow the shore around to the left and you come to a low bridge decked in summer with boxes of geraniums and petunias. From here you can enjoy the antics of people in the rowing boats which can be hired nearby. The water is now just 4 feet deep; it has been kept shallow since 1867, when forty skaters drowned after falling through thin ice.

North-west of the lake are two buildings attached to two culturally opposed worlds: the mosque (**30**), with its gleaming bronze dome and towering minaret, completed in 1977, and, slightly uphill, Winfield, a neo-Georgian villa which is now the residence of the American ambassador. Regent's Canal flows behind.

Take the path between the lake and the children's boating pond and make for the sports fields. To the west are strange barren rocks in the distance. These are the Goat Hills belonging to the zoo, of which you can get many glimpses from the park. When the zoo first opened (it was founded in 1826) keepers insisted that horsewhips should be left outside and that overwrought ladies must refrain from poking the animals with their parasols. Today visitors are a little more civilised and can see about 8,000 beasts and beauties here.

Behind the zoo rise the 42 acres of Primrose Hill, which can be reached by a path leading up from the road outside Lord Snowdon's Aviary. From the hill's summit (206 feet) you can, on a clear day, see to the south the Telecom Tower, St Paul's, Westminster Abbey and sometimes even the distant Surrey and Kent hills. There are no primroses here now, but a mild December brings the pink blossom of Winter-Flowering Cherry trees.

In the 17th century the hill – then known as Greenbury Hill – was a favourite spot for duelling. The Crown acquired it in 1842 and curbed its wildness with paths and street lamps. Samuel Phelps, an actor, planted an oak near the foot of the hill in 1864 to celebrate Shakespeare's tercentenary, but the land was too boggy and the sapling died. One hundred years later the Society for Theatre Research planted another, which happily survives. The hill is a fine open space and long may it continue to be so, for in the 18th century a prophetess, Mother Shipton, made a terrible prediction: when London surrounds Primrose Hill, the streets of the metropolis will run with blood.

32 *Regent's Park zoo in winter: a wombat in the snow. Despite the bars shown here, efforts are made to avoid cages wherever possible; moats surrounding the large-animal pens allow unrestricted views of the inhabitants.*

31 *Queen Mary's
Gardens, Regent's Park,
were laid out by the Royal
Botanic Society, which
leased the site from 1840
to 1932. The small statue
is* Boy with a Frog *by
Sir William Reid Dick
(1936).*

OVERLEAF
33 *Woodland in
Richmond Park, a view
which suggests the park's
great expanse. The
characteristically English
selection of trees includes
oak, hornbeam, beech and
Horse Chestnut.*

Richmond Park

> 'Ye, who from London's smoke and turmoil fly
> To seek a purer and a brighter sky . . .'

The 18th-century poet James Thomson wrote this invocation, which is found on a huge board in the Pembroke Lodge gardens of Richmond Park. Having trekked out to Richmond (not London proper, but Surrey), you are under at least a more open sky, for the park is part of a spread of unbroken country which includes Petersham Meadows and the commons of Ham, East Sheen and Wimbledon. It has thousands of indigenous trees and 2,358 undulating acres, making it the largest of all the royal parks. Coppices and stretches of bracken cover ground virtually unchanged since the 17th century, and there are herds of deer which roam unaware that they are a major tourist attraction.

Richmond, perhaps because of its remoter location, escaped the civilising mania which transformed hunting grounds into royal gardens. There are no fountains or statues, though flowers do make a guest appearance. Walking here you are exploring old English countryside. And walk you must. The road swinging around the edge of the park helps establish a sense of direction, but it is no good trying to sightsee from a car; you will miss the hidden charms of the park. Even at night, the pedestrian gates stay open.

Shene or Schene, home to Henry I, was the first manor connected with the area. It was burnt down in the 14th century, rebuilt, destroyed again and then resurrected in the 15th century by Henry VII, who named it after his title, Earl

43

of Richmond. All that is left of Richmond Palace is an archway and the Palace Gate House, on Richmond Green.

It was the profligate Charles I who created the park. He hankered after seclusion, thinking the existing royal parks were too near the centre of London, and he sequestered land from local owners, who had no choice but to sell. Even the Chancellor of the Exchequer warned against so rash a course, knowing that the London citizens would object to paying more taxes to meet the cost. Charles, however, continued and raised a brick wall (still in existence though partially rebuilt) around his hunting ground, which he called 'New Park', a name surviving until the close of the 19th century. He may have been reckless, but at least he allowed the public a right of way through the park and permission to dig gravel and gather firewood. Today hardly anyone collects fuel, but in October gourmets armed with carrier bags forage for sweet chestnuts. After the King's execution in 1649 the New Park was presented to the citizens of London, who preyed on and rapidly destroyed the deer (even today the herds are culled, and haunches of venison find their way to the tables of royalty and dignitaries), but when Charles II acquired the throne the citizens had the good sense to return his father's land to him.

Public access became severely restricted under the Hanoverians. George II appointed his Prime Minister Sir Robert Walpole as Park Ranger, and Walpole began restoring the park to its former glory. He even introduced flocks of wild turkeys so that the King could hunt without over-exerting himself. (The poor birds were chased into the trees, where they could be shot easily.) The White

34 *A bed of brilliantly coloured dahlias in the Pembroke Lodge gardens, Richmond Park. Although in origin a Mexican plant, the dahlia takes its name from a Swedish botanist called Dahl. The first dahlias in Europe were grown in Madrid's Royal Gardens in 1789; they were introduced into England in 1804.*

35 *Woodland in Richmond Park. When Charles I enclosed the area to create what was then called the 'New Park', it was waste ground and commonland interspersed with property belonging to the Crown and to other people, who were forced to sell up. It had always been used for sport – Henry VIII is known to have hunted here. The park contains approximately 20,000 trees, mostly indigenous species.*

Lodge was built in 1727 as a 'hunting box' for George, and he and the Queen would take tea here on Sunday afternoons. Sometimes she would canter along the track which leads from the building and is now known as the Queen's Ride.

Sir Robert, having invested time and money in the park, discouraged the public by closing the gates and removing ladders which gave access over the walls – a practice continued by the next Ranger, Princess Amelia, aunt to George III. This determined lady moved into the White Lodge in 1751. She hoped to keep the public out altogether by employing a beefy gatekeeper, Deborah Burgess, to dissuade them from entering. A tradesman, John Lewis, brought a charge against Amelia, basing his case on the rights of way granted by Charles I. Within a month ladder-stiles were erected by order of the judge. But the Princess was not so easily defeated: she had ladders fitted with rungs spaced so widely apart that only the agile could use them. John Lewis returned to court and forced the Princess to supply suitable gates. He became a local hero and Amelia sold the rangership to her nephew.

Wandering freely is a sensible way to tackle a park this size. If you want to see some of the 400 fallow and 300 red deer, they seem to collect, somewhat surprisingly, near the roads. You can enter the park by any one of the six carriage or five pedestrian gates but the main one at Richmond with its letters GR and CR (King George II and Queen Charlotte) might be best. Cycling is a good way to get about, but if you are travelling by car, leave it in the free car park by Pembroke Lodge (follow the signs for Ham Gate). This elegant white building began life as a molecatcher's cottage and later became the grace-and-favour home of Lord John (Earl) Russell. His orphaned grandson, the great philosopher Bertrand Russell, was brought up here. Inside Pembroke Lodge are a café and restaurant. From the rear of the building, on a clear day, you can look across the wide valley and see the blue Chilterns of Oxfordshire. The garden (**34**) falls away in a series of terraces flush with Ericas, which should be seen in winter or early spring. The steep path descends to Petersham Park and the river meadows. (You can walk to Ham House this way; see pp. 83–5.)

Keeping Petersham Meadows on your left, follow the path north and it will take you to the highest point in Richmond Park: Henry VIII's Mound. Tradition relates how Henry scaled the hill to watch for a rocket signal fired from the Tower of London which told him his second wife, Anne Boleyn, had been beheaded, leaving him free to marry the third. It is possibly an ancient burial ground. With the hill behind you, continue northwards and enjoy the Laburnum walk (in May) and quit Pembroke Lodge gardens by the gate.

Sidmouth Wood – the largest in the park – lies opposite. Planting began here in 1823 with the introduction of oaks, beeches and Sweet Chestnuts. As it is a bird sanctuary most of the wood is closed to walkers, but you can stroll through the centre along the Driftway, which runs east–west. Cross the road, bear right and follow the edge of the wood round. On your left you pass one locked gate; the second may look locked but it is not. On either side of the path tower huge rhododendron bushes, which flower in June.

Leaving the wood, head for the Pen Ponds. These lie at the bottom of a wide grassy track which slopes away to your left. Once gravel pits, they were formed by Princess Amelia and accommodate pink roach, carp and gudgeon. Keen birdwatchers might spot a kestrel, kingfisher, or woodpecker as well as the resident coot, mallard and heron.

Stick to the gravelly path between the upper and lower pond and make for Spankers Hill Wood, where an uphill road to the left brings you to the White Lodge, now home of the Royal Ballet School. When George III's Prime Minister Henry Addington was tenant here, Admiral Lord Nelson was one of many famous guests. He dined here six weeks before the Battle of Trafalgar and supposedly traced out on a table top with a finger wet with wine the plan he intended to use to defeat the French. Queen Victoria also spent time in the lodge with an aunt who lived here, and Victoria's great-grandson Edward VIII was born in one of the rooms.

Turn away from the house and the hideous Roehampton tower blocks on the horizon, return to Spankers Hill and follow the path back via the car park to the Isabella Plantation (**37**) on the left. The Isabella might appear to be an uninteresting clump of dark trees but it should not be missed. Since 1951 it has been a woodland garden with the most comprehensive collection of azaleas you could ever wish to see, resplendent in May or early June. If possible view them on an overcast day, when their vividness and scent are strongest. Two artificial ponds and a stream keep the garden watered; there is also a heather garden, which comes into its own in February and March, and a camellia walk. Japanese Maples, Weeping Willows, oaks and beeches tower above rhododendrons, foxgloves and irises, so that you make your way beneath a lavish canopy of green.

The Thatched House Lodge (1727) is south-west of the plantation. No longer thatched, but with climbing roses and shutters which give it a slightly Spanish air, it is situated between the Ham and Kingston Gates and since 1963 has been the home of Princess Alexandra and her husband, Angus Ogilvy.

36 *Richmond Park is especially beautiful in autumn, as the bracken starts to turn red-gold, the chestnuts lose their fruit and the leaves take on brilliant colours.*

Hampton Court and Bushy Park

Hampton Court '. . . is as noble and uniform a pile and as capacious as any Gothic architecture can have made it', wrote John Evelyn in 1662. Today, whether you approach Hampton Court by river or by road, the magnificence is still striking. Only 13 miles from central London, the palace is surrounded by just under 2,000 acres, of which its gardens account for 669. To the north lies Bushy Park; to the east Hampton Court Park; and the Thames winds its way along the southern boundary.

Modified over the years to suit the requirements of a succession of patrons, Hampton Court has grown from the grand provincial home of an ambitious 16th-century prelate to the palatial residence of 17th- and 18th-century kings, its gracious gardens revised several times according to the fashion of the day. In the 13th century a manor house which belonged to the Knights Hospitallers of St John of Jerusalem stood here. In 1514 Cardinal Wolsey, accompanied by Henry VIII, came on a visit. This enormously wealthy and powerful priest was looking for a quiet country retreat and lighted on Hampton Court. He bought it, divided the land into two parks, fashioned gardens and fenced in his property. As the King began to find fault with the worldly cardinal, Wolsey attempted to ingratiate himself with Henry by giving him the use of the house. Four years later, with characteristic lack of gratitude, the King took complete possession, dividing up the parks and stocking them with deer. The fallow herd in Bushy Park is said to be descended from his original game.

When the King arrived at Hampton Court by river he would land south-west

37 *The Isabella Plantation in Richmond Park contains one of the country's most comprehensive collections of azaleas, although they were not introduced to the plantation until 1951. At their best from early May to June, their red, orange, pink, white and coral-coloured flowers make a magical display.*

of the palace at the Water Gallery, a passage which led through the gardens. Where the Privy Garden is now he formed the Pond Garden, with a mount at one end topped by a summer-house with a superb view of the river. Winding its way to the summit was a path made of crushed cockleshells bordered with rosemary and marked out by heraldic beasts on posts painted in the Tudor green and white. Running along the western edge was an arched alley of hornbeams: Queen Anne's Bower, named after Anne Boleyn. The hornbeams have been replaced with Wych Elms and it is now known as Queen Mary's Bower, after William III's wife, who liked to sit here and sew. North-east of the palace Henry introduced tilt-yards, erecting five spectator towers, one of which survives, adapted as a restaurant. Imagine how gorgeous the scene must have been with the swaggering jousters in white damask and silver cloth.

Though Charles II spent his honeymoon here he was not enamoured of the place – perhaps because his father had been interned here during the Civil War, or because Cromwell had commandeered the palace for his home. Despite this the grounds owe their form largely to Charles. An admirer of French formal gardens, he imagined Hampton Court as an English Versailles. His gardener John Rose was a pupil of the landscape designer Le Nôtre (see above, p. 11). And so the flat, featureless land near the palace was laid out with a dazzling display of formal avenues and ornamental water. Three avenues of Dutch lime trees were planted radiating out in a *patte d'oie* (goosefoot) pattern from the east front. The central line consisted of a Dutch-style canal running between the trees for three-quarters of a mile into Hampton Court Park. The basic ground-plan of this design remains.

38 *The east front of Hampton Court, seen from Broad Walk. This is part of the extension to the original Tudor palace; it was designed by Christopher Wren and built 1689–94. This range is occupied by the Queen's apartments. The trees are yew.*

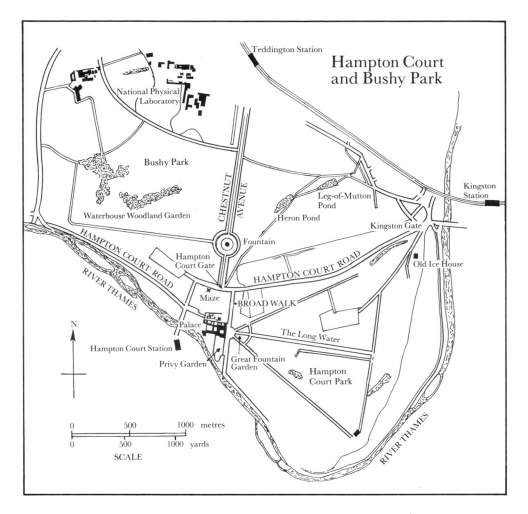

William III liked the park because its flatness reminded him of his homeland, Holland. Christopher Wren extended the palace greatly and William restyled Charles's *patte d'oie* as the Great Fountain Garden. The semicircular shape remained but miniature hedges of clipped box scrollwork were introduced and beds were edged with yews trimmed into small obelisks. In the centre spurted a jet of water from a round basin with twelve supporting fountains. A Wilderness – a formal garden of evergreens in geometric patterns – took the place of the tilt-yards, and the half-mile Broad Walk on the eastern front was laid out and decorated with orange trees symbolising William's descent from the House of Orange. Henry's Mount disappeared; so did the Water Gallery, which was replaced by the castellated banqueting hall you can see today.

Queen Anne, who liked neither her brother-in-law, nor Hampton Court, nor the smell of box, had William's design modified after his death. Thirteen fountains became five (and, much later, one), while the box topiary made way for rolling lawns and gravel paths. A red-brick orangery was built, the maze was planted and a 'chaise-riding' (a system of levelled tracks) was set out in Hampton Court Park so that the plump and gouty Queen could join in the hunt, riding in a gig. The superb herbaceous beds on Broad Walk were laid out in the 18th century, when grassy slopes superseded the steps in the Privy

OVERLEAF

40 *The Long Water, a ¾-mile-long ornamental canal, was constructed for Charles II in imitation of the formal magnificence of Versailles. It is the most spectacular feature of Hampton Court Park and even in winter boasts a stark grandeur. This view is from the Great Fountain Garden.*

39 *One of the two magnificent 17th-century wrought-iron gates by Jean Tijou which separate the Great Fountain Garden from Hampton Court Park. Tijou is best known for his superb wrought-iron screens in St Paul's Cathedral.*

Garden and the Great Vine was planted. Queen Victoria opened Hampton Court to the public in 1837, the year of her coronation.

Every year about 1,500,000 people visit the gardens, so you will not be alone as you venture into Broad Walk and the Great Fountain Garden (see map). Ahead stretches the Long Water (**40**) with its white swans and water-lilies. Over the years the pyramidal yews have turned cone-shaped (**41**) and it takes two gardeners a day and a half to prune each one. (Ninety-nine gardeners look after the parks and gardens here.) Hampton Court Park stretches away to the east behind Jean Tijou's two gates (**39**, at the bottom of the Great Fountain Garden) and its trees include Lombardy Poplars and a Turkey Oak, the tallest tree in Hampton Court.

As you emerge from the palace, turn right, along Broad Walk, and right again through a gateway into the Privy Garden, which has a raised terrace leading south to Jean Tijou's sumptuous 17th-century screen. Consisting of twelve panels with heraldic motifs, it separates the garden from the towpath. Among the lilacs and luxuriant magnolias look out for the Judas and Kentucky Coffee Trees.

The Knot and Pond Gardens no longer have true Tudor plants. Knot gardens, always designed to be seen from state apartments, are so called because the low dense hedges of thyme, rosemary or Dwarf Box seem to tie themselves into writhing contortions within the formal square. In the past, beds were crammed with lavenders, pinks and wallflowers; today you will find lobelias, begonias and heliotropes. The Knot Garden is on the right of the path; opposite is the

Pond Garden, garlanded with pleached limes and wisteria along the 16th-century walls. Rising up behind is the roof of the banqueting house.

The building at the end of the path houses the largest Black Hamburg Vine in Britain. Planted in 1768, this gnarled monster has thousands of offshoots and, at its stem, a girth of 7 feet. Some branches are 114 feet long and every year it yields about 700 lb of grapes, which are on sale at the end of August. The brick building to the right is Queen Anne's Orangery, where you can pay to see Mantegna's series of paintings *The Triumph of Caesar* (*c.* 1486–94).

Back again on Broad Walk, head north towards Flower Pot Gate (1699), adorned with figures of putti by John Nost. On the left, before you reach the gate, are Henry VIII's indoor tennis courts. Real (or royal) tennis, based on the French game *jeu de paume*, uses a solid ball which is hit against the walls of the court as in squash rackets. You may see a game in progress.

A gate further along leads to the Wilderness, an area swamped with daffodils in spring. The peace of the rose garden, part of the Wilderness, replaces the heaves and grunts of past jousts, and beyond, through a door in the wall, you will find a secret garden with luxuriant flower-beds. The famous Maze is also part of the Wilderness. Its original hornbeam hedges are now mixed with privet and yew. Children always enjoy trying to get lost inside and a fee is charged for the privilege.

Walk in the direction of the Maze and Hampton Court Gate with the Laburnum Walk on your right and cross the busy Hampton Court Road for the 1,100 acres of Bushy Park. In the 17th century Sir Christopher Wren turned this heathland into a grand processional route leading to the north front of the

41 *The huge yew trees in the Great Fountain Garden of Hampton Court began life as trim obelisks drawing the eye down a vista towards the Long Water. Today these 'black pyramids', as Virginia Woolf described them, are over 30 feet high.*

42 *The Waterhouse Woodland Gardens, in Bushy Park, are watered by an artificial stream channelled from the Colne in Charles I's time. Famous for its azaleas and rhododendrons, it is also a bird sanctuary: if you are lucky you might spot a willow warbler, whitethroat or spotted flycatcher here.*

palace. The 60-foot-wide road running through the centre of the park is flanked for a mile by two rows of limes on each side, with a row of chestnuts in between them. May is the time to visit, when the Roman candles on the Horse Chestnuts are out. Breaking the avenue is a fountain with a figure of Arethusa, often mistakenly called Diana, looking rather abashed by her isolated position on top of a high pedestal. Sculpted by Francesco Fanelli for Charles I, she was originally placed in the Privy Garden.

In 1638 Charles I redirected the Longford river, a tributary of the Colne, across Hounslow Heath to feed the Hampton Court gardens. It also flows into the charming Waterhouse Woodland Gardens (**42**). (Follow the avenue north; the gardens are signposted on your left as you enter the park.) These 100 or so acres provide a bird sanctuary and a cool green oasis in summer. The planting of rhododendrons and azaleas, begun in 1949, looks as natural as possible. Swamp Cypresses, Tulip Trees and Water Firs are dwarfed by a 138-foot-high London Plane. The Heron and Leg-of-Mutton Ponds lie east of the park. The public right of way near them was preserved after a legal battle fought by one Timothy Bennet, shoemaker, in the 18th century. Few people seem to bother with the west part of Bushy Park, but if you want to get away from the crowds around Hampton Court and seek some scenic solitude, there is no more attractive place to do so.

Working Gardens

The Royal Botanic Gardens, Kew

There is still something of the private garden about Kew, secure behind high brick walls and the ha-ha which separates it from the river. It is not just that visitors must pay a token fee to wander among the vistas and lakes; as a scientific institution the gardens also work for their living – the herbarium, library and laboratory are there to serve botanists and horticulturists. But amateurs too can stroll among the 50,000 to 60,000 species, including many rare or even unique specimens, and visit the museums and permanent exhibition. For the general visitor the 300 acres offer unrivalled beauty and tranquillity.

At one time Kew Gardens were divided between three properties, only one of which – the Dutch House, also known as Kew Palace (**44**) – survives, in the north-west corner. The second, Richmond or Ormonde Lodge, was adopted as a summer residence in the 1720s by George II, who employed Charles Bridgeman to plant the grounds and William Kent to furnish them with follies. Lodge and garden buildings were later demolished, as was the third property, the White House, which was leased to George II's son Frederick, Prince of Wales, and his wife, Augusta. Widowed prematurely, Augusta began gathering exotic greenery for a 9-acre botanic garden, the nucleus of the present collection. She asked William Chambers (co-founder of the Royal Academy) to create some garden buildings. Three of his six miniature classical temples survive, as do his mock Roman bridge and orangery. Chambers, who had travelled to China, also designed the tall pagoda (**43**) with its ten storeys and projecting roofs. The eighty enamelled dragons which once decorated the structure have gone, as have Chambers' mosque and alhambra which flanked it.

On the death of his grandfather and mother, George III inherited both Ormonde Lodge and the White House and united their grounds, which were modified by Capability Brown. Sir Joseph Banks was appointed horticultural advisor, and he introduced many foreign species to Kew. On George's death, the gardens were neglected until 1841, when they were given to the nation. Sir William Hooker, the first Director, was succeeded by his son Joseph; between them they initiated the Department of Economic Botany and opened several museums here, confirming Kew as a centre of horticultural education in a setting of unparalleled richness and diversity.

The following suggested route (see map) takes in the main areas of interest: the Queen's Garden, the Temperate and Palm Houses, the lake, the Pagoda and Queen Charlotte's Cottage grounds. Enter the gardens from Kew Green by the impressive main gates, designed by Decimus Burton (1845–6). The first stop, right of Broad Walk, is John Nash's Aroid House, originally one of two garden pavilions built for Buckingham Palace but re-erected here in 1836 to

43 *Kew's famous Pagoda was designed by Sir William Chambers for Princess Augusta in 1761–2, when chinoiserie was a fashionable style for garden buildings. Chambers had travelled to China as a member of the Swedish East India Company; he later wrote a very influential essay on oriental gardening. The Pagoda is 163 feet high (ten storeys) and was once decorated with glass dragons in dazzling colours; it is said that George IV sold them to pay his debts. The Pagoda's flimsy construction (it took only six months to erect) means that it cannot be opened to the public.*

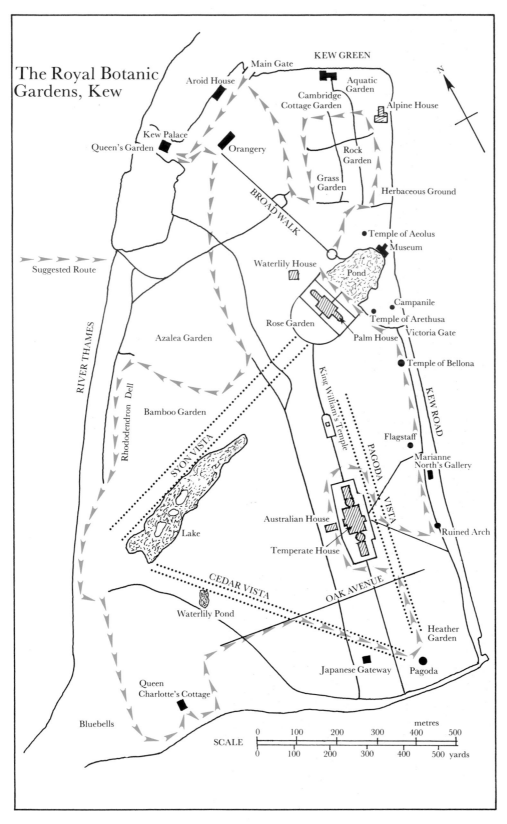

The Royal Botanic Gardens, Kew

KEW GREEN

Main Gate

Aroid House

Aquatic Garden

Cambridge Cottage Garden

Alpine House

Kew Palace

Queen's Garden

Orangery

Rock Garden

Grass Garden

Herbaceous Ground

BROAD WALK

Temple of Aeolus

Museum

Waterlily House

Pond

Suggested Route

Campanile

Rose Garden

Temple of Arethusa

Victoria Gate

Palm House

Azalea Garden

Temple of Bellona

RIVER THAMES

Rhododendron Dell

Bamboo Garden

King William's Temple

KEW ROAD

Flagstaff

SYON VISTA

PAGODA VISTA

Marianne North's Gallery

Lake

Australian House

Ruined Arch

Temperate House

CEDAR VISTA

OAK AVENUE

Waterlily Pond

Heather Garden

Queen Charlotte's Cottage

Japanese Gateway

Pagoda

Bluebells

metres

SCALE

0   100   200   300   400   500

0   100   200   300   400   500 yards

44 *Kew Palace, seen here from the Queen's Garden, was built for a merchant, Samuel Fortrey, in 1631 on the foundations of a 16th-century building called the Dairy House. It was acquired by George III; his wife, Queen Charlotte, died here in 1818, when it ceased to be a royal residence. In the centre of the garden, a reconstruction containing only plants grown in the 17th century, is a Venetian well-head with a modern wrought-iron top.*

OVERLEAF
45 *Swathes of bluebells cover the 37 acres of Queen Charlotte's Cottage grounds, Kew, once part of the grounds of Ormonde Lodge. The semi-wild gardens were presented to Kew Gardens by Queen Victoria in 1897 and opened to the public two years later; they are a sanctuary for many species of wild birds.*

house plants from the lower levels of the tropical rain forest. Broad Walk branches off on the left, but take the narrower path straight ahead, which leads to Kew Palace.

This beautiful 17th-century brick mansion was built for the merchant Samuel Fortrey and his wife, Catherine, and their initials are in the brickwork above the main entrance, with the date 1631. It became a royal home in the late 18th century. If you do not wish to enter, take the path to the right of the palace, which leads into the formal and peaceful Queen's Garden (**44**). This runs

between the palace and the river and is divided into three parts. Straight ahead of you, a narrow avenue is lined on either side by hornbeam hedges clipped to look as though they are on stilts. It leads to a mound, scaled by a zig-zag path cut through box and crowned by a modern gilded gazebo. Directly behind the mansion is the parterre, a geometrical layout of dense Dwarf Box hedges and beds of lavender, ornamental sage and rosemary. Further to the west is the sunken Nosegay Garden, bordered on three sides by a pleached Laburnum walk, magnificent in May. Here grow the herbs and scented flowers that would have been used in the 17th century for posies, in medicines, or as fragrant clippings strewn on floors. A low box hedge surrounds beds packed with Wormwood (*Artemisia absinthium*), Double-Flowered Camomile (*Anthemis nobilis*), Germander (*Teucrium chamaedrys*) and Sea Ragweed (*Sencio bicolor*), as well as Heartsease, pinks and Mignonette. At the river end of the sunken part note the low bench, its seat sown with camomile.

Return to Broad Walk. The orangery (now a bookstall and exhibition hall) is

46 *Kew's huge Temperate House was designed by Decimus Burton and took nearly forty years to build (1860–99). It is a long rectangular structure with north and south wings linked to a main building by octagonal vestibules. It was intended primarily as a winter garden and is designed so that the roof can be opened in hot weather.*

immediately to the left; concealed behind it is the Filmy Fern House. Recross Broad Walk, and follow the signs for the lake. Turn right at the sign for the Bamboo Garden. To your right is the Azalea Garden, laid out over a hundred years ago and flooded with colour in May and June. Beyond spread the exotic Bamboo Garden and the Rhododendron Dell, designed by Capability Brown as the 'Hollow Walk'. Many flamboyant species were introduced here when Joseph Hooker returned with them from his travels in the Himalayas (1848–51).

You emerge into the magnificent Syon Vista, whose mighty Holm Oaks run east–west alongside these gardens. Stand with your back to the distant Palm House in the east for a fine view of Syon House across the river (see pp. 102–7). Syon Vista runs parallel to the artificial lake, created in the last century. Boathouse Walk, on the opposite shore, is marked by trees from the Old World on its southern side, and by trees from the New on the other. One, the Dawn Redwood Tree (*Metasequoia glyptostroboides*), was discovered in China in 1941, thought until then to have been extinct for a hundred million years.

At the head of the lake pause to look south down Cedar Vista, which culminates in the Pagoda. Turn right and take the path running near the river into the grounds of Queen Charlotte's Cottage, in May a sea of bluebells (**45**). Queen Victoria presented these 37 acres to the nation on her Diamond Jubilee, stipulating that they should remain in their semi-wild state. The thatched wood cottage was built *c.* 1772 and was supposedly designed by Queen Charlotte, George III's wife, as a picnic site, and the rooms do seem created for effect rather than convenience:

Leaving this enclave, join Oak Avenue. Among the interesting trees on either side are rare Nutmegs, Chinese Fir (*Cunninghamia lanceolata*) and Umbrella Pine (*Sciadopitys verticillata*). Not far from the Pagoda perches 'The Gateway of the Imperial Messenger' (Chokushi-Mon), installed here in 1910, and modelled on a 16th-century temple gateway in Kyoto, Japan. Countering all this oriental whimsy is the rugged Heather Garden, between the Pagoda and the road, glorious from September to October and from February to March.

North of the Pagoda is the Australian House with its endemic collection, while just in front stands the splendid Temperate House (**46**; 1860–99), designed by Decimus Burton. It covers an area of 628 feet × 137 feet 6 inches – twice the size of the Palm House. Once known as the Winter Garden, its rare treasures include a Cretan Date Palm, a leathery-leaved *Elingatnita johnsonii* from New Zealand and the colossal Chilean Wine Palm (*Jubaea chilensis*), nurtured from a seed in 1846 and now 58 feet high. Tucked into one corner is the gorgeously coloured Bird of Paradise Flower, or *Strelitzia reginae*, a name honouring Queen Charlotte of the House of Mecklenburg Strelitz. This par-

47 *The Palm House, Kew, was built 1844–8 and houses a wide variety of tropical plants. The palms are mostly in the north wing and central area, where there is room for growth – for a palm cannot survive cutting back, and once it reaches the roof its life is over. The terrace in front of the Palm House is a modification of the original parterre designed in 1847 by W.A. Nesfield; it incorporates the Queen's Beasts (see frontispiece).*

ticular plant is descended from one brought back from southern Africa in 1773.

A path north of the building leads through the mixed shrubs to King William IV's temple, its interior decked with plaques commemorating battles fought between 1760 and 1815. Double back along Pagoda Vista to join the path skirting the edge of the park, by Kew Road. Here you pass through Chambers' Ruined Arch with its casually tumbled stones and can see Marianne North's Gallery with her 848 oil paintings of flora and fauna, the fruits of this Victorian traveller's excursions around the world. By the path towers the 225-foot flag-staff made from a single Douglas Fir and presented by the Government of British Columbia. Further along sits the Temple of Bellona, the ground around it a carpet of crocuses in spring. A second building, the Temple of Arethusa, appears on the other side of Victoria Gate, together with Burton's 'campanile' – a water-tower and once also a chimney for the furnaces originally under the Palm House. The Temple of Aeolus, set in the woodland garden, completes Chambers' trio of temples; it possessed a revolving seat until renovated by Decimus Burton. See it in spring in a crowd of daffodils.

Now make for the Palm House (**47**), a masterpiece of Victorian engineering. Designed by Decimus Burton and Richard Turner (1844–8), it is 362 feet long, and 62 feet high in the centre, its frame a triumph of wrought iron. Inside you will discover *Encephalartos longifolius*, probably the oldest living greenhouse plant in Kew, transported from southern Africa in 1775. But the most unusual inmate must be *E. woodii*, a cycad from Zululand which arrived in Kew thirteen years before becoming extinct in the wild (1918), an offset from the only male plant ever known.

48 *The building on the far side of the lake from the Palm House is the Museum of Economically Useful Plants (for example those grown for rubber, dye and oil), designed by Decimus Burton and opened in 1857. Fine Swamp Cypresses grow around the lake. The statue,* Hercules Fighting, *by F.J. Bosio, was cast for Windsor Castle in 1826, and was presented to Kew by the Queen in 1962.*

At the back of the Palm House is the Rose Garden, with attendant cone-shaped holly trees; at the front is a terrace (frontispiece) furnished with a line of ten Queen's Beasts (replicas of 16th-century heraldic emblems carved in 1953 for Elizabeth II's coronation). Two Chinese Guardian Lions snarl at the fountain figure of Hercules stationed in the large pond. Facing the Palm House, on the other side of the pond, stands the Museum for Economically Useful Plants (**48**).

Across the path, Decimus Burton's Tropical Waterlily House of 1852 was built for the Giant Amazon Waterlily (*Victoria amazonica*), introduced in 1849. The lily's enormous leaves grow to 6 feet in diameter and can support a 150 lb weight. The flowers, which appear from July to October, turn from white to purple but last only two days. Also of interest here is the Sacred Bean Lotus (*Nelumbo nucifera*), from India, characterised by large waxy leaves and ravishing pink flowers.

The specialist gardens group in a cluster in the north-east corner of the park. The walled Herbaceous Ground, once a kitchen garden, displays families of plants and a rose pergola. Next to it is the Alpine Rock Garden, laid out in 1882 – see it in late May. To the west thrive the succulents and the ferns, and trees planted by Princess Augusta: Maidenhair Tree (*Ginkgo biloba*), False Acacia (*Robinia pseudoacacia*) and Pagoda Tree (*Sophora japonica*), all saplings in 1761. North of the Rock Garden are the Iris and Acquatic Gardens and the Alpine House, which simulates high mountain conditions for its residents.

Towards the river is the Cambridge Cottage (or Duke's) Garden (**49**), in front of the house, now a wood museum, where once the Duke of Cambridge lived. Dotted between the colourful herbaceous beds are rarities like the Iron

49 *Herbaceous plants in Cambridge Cottage Garden, Kew. This beautiful walled garden is also known as 'The Duke's Garden' after the Dukes of Cambridge, who once lived in the house that can be seen on the left in the distance. On the death of the second duke in 1904, the house and its grounds became part of the Royal Botanic Gardens – the last royal property to be absorbed into Kew. The house was converted into a wood museum in 1910.*

Tree (*Parrotia persica*) from Persia and the Chinese Gutta Percha Tree (*Eucommia ulmoides*) which produces rubber in its leaves.

Along the south-facing wall stretches the Duchess's Border, where tender flowers grow: South African nerines and *Sophora microphylla*, native to New Zealand – the remotest point from which any plant has travelled to Kew. Notice also the rare Chinese conifer *Thuja orientalis*. Before leaving this area do stop at the Grass Garden. Did you realise quite how many kinds there are of this common or garden plant?

Chelsea Physic Garden and the Royal Hospital Gardens, Chelsea

Founded in 1673 by the Worshipful Society of Apothecaries, Chelsea Physic Garden was established for the study and cultivation of plants for medical purposes. It is the oldest botanic garden in England after Oxford, and had already been thriving for a hundred years when Kew was still primarily a landscape garden.

Seventeenth-century walls enclose 4 acres cut off from the river on the south side by the Embankment. The fine houses of Swan Walk run along the east side and it is here you enter the garden, through the original wrought-iron Students' Gates. The garden is open on Wednesday and Sunday afternoons from April to October.

It was the benevolence of Sir Hans Sloane, President of the Royal College of Physicians, which allowed the garden to survive. In 1712 he bought the Manor of Chelsea, which included this garden, and ten years later he gave the Apothecaries a lease in perpetuity for £5 a year rent. In return they had to use the garden for research, and send 50 specimens to the Royal Society annually until 2,000 species had been preserved. A statue of Sir Hans (**50**) sits in the centre of the garden, a copy of one by Michael Rysbrack commissioned in 1733 and now on permanent loan to the British Museum.

At Sir Hans's suggestion, Philip Miller (1691–1771) took on the curatorship of the garden and became one of the greatest horticulturists of his day. An orangery-cum-greenhouse was designed at his instigation, with a library and meeting rooms above and heated greenhouses on either side, but in the late 19th century all this was swept away. It was a black period for the Physic Garden, as botany began to play a less important role in medical research. London pollution, too, was taking its toll, and the Embankment had reduced the level of the water-table, leaving the soil poorly nourished. Staff were laid off and the Apothecaries discussed selling the land for redevelopment. Fortunately the Charity Commissioners stepped in and the garden was handed over to several bodies working under the Trustees of the London Parochial Charities. The management passed to a new body of independent Trustees in 1983. The garden has welcomed the public since then, while sustaining its educational and scientific roles.

Many of the 5,000 species here are the result of exchanges with gardens abroad. John Watts, a 17th-century curator, brought back from Leiden four Lebanon Cedars, perhaps the first to be grown in this country. By 1771 two had been felled because they had absorbed too much space; the last survived until 1904. In the late 18th century, Sir Joseph Banks, President of the Royal Society, introduced not only new plants but also Icelandic basaltic lava to create the earliest rock garden in England, in an attempt to rear in the right ecological conditions the plants he had collected. It was supplemented with stone brought from the Tower of London by the head gardener, William Forsyth, after whom the glorious yellow shrub Forsythia is named. Another of Banks's gifts was *Sophora tetraptera*, related to the 'Kowhai', New Zealand's national flower. The one growing by the north exit is a descendant of the original, brought back from Captain Cook's first voyage on the *Endeavour*. Plants have also been sent around the world from Chelsea: in 1734 a botanic garden in Georgia received the cotton seeds which made so many fortunes in the deep South.

As you leave the gate, take the path to your left, which leads towards the river. The area stretching away to your right is one of systematic order beds, which comprise one third of the garden. It houses the families Ranunculaceae to Rosaceae (section one of the Dicotyledons). Among the unusual herbaceous perennials look out for the clear blue flowers of the *Delphinium tatsienense*, which blossoms in May. Towering above the neat rows is a Chinese Willow Pattern Tree (*Koelreuteria paniculata*), the best example in Britain and one which perhaps inspired 18th-century decorators of porcelain.

An old *Styrax officinalis* and *Buxus balearica* grow further along. Follow the path round, and to your right you will find a vast Holm Oak (*Quercus ilex*) beneath which burgeon heathers, dwarf rhododendrons and Himalayan primulas. South American plants, including two species of *Colletia* from Argentina, are tucked into this south-east corner. Notable among tender subtropical plants from this region are the salvia species from Mexico and fragrant Chilean Jasmine (*Mandevilla laxa*), with its creamy flowers.

Keep to this path. From April to June wild peonies, among them the *Paeonia cambessedesii* from the Balearic Islands, flower in the mixed shrub area to the left. A path strikes off right, but keep to the one you are on, flanked by the Hypericum collection on the left and a pool edged with pink Flowering Rush (*Butomus umbellatus*) and blue pickerel weed (*Pontederia cordata*) on the right. A Dawn Redwood hangs over the water. On the far side of the pool extend the Californian Borders with their white poppies (*Romneya trichocalyx*), and further ahead still, the second set of systematic order beds of Dicotyledons (Lythraceae to Labiatae). Of special interest here are the rare *Echium rubrum*, a pyramid of scarlet flowers in May, and *Centaurea ruthenica alba*, which blooms a month later.

Guarding the path by the Swamp Cypress are two Maidenhair Trees. After you pass the Embankment Gates, spreading to your right are the systematic order beds of Monocotyledons (Iridaceae to Gramineae). Spot the Foxtail Lilies (*Eremurus*) – yellow *bungei*, white *himalaicus*, peach-coloured *robustus* – and the spring-flowering sky-blue blooms of the Grape Hyacinth (*Muscari botryoides*), introduced to the garden by Philip Miller. Prominent here is the Chusan Palm (*Trachycarpus fortunei*), a native of South China and uncommon in this country.

The path leads north, passing the midwinter Mimosa (*Acacia dealbata*), whose golden flowers brighten bleak February, the Australian plants along the western wall and the Historic Garden and the Chinese Border. Turn right towards the statue of Sir Hans. A Cucumber Tree (*Magnolia acuminata*), which bears shocking pink fruit in autumn, appears just before you reach the rock gardens on the left. The woodland area (at its best between October and April) is to your right. The path on the left of the statue leads to the greenhouses, where you can examine the Madagascan Periwinkle (*Catharanthus roseus*), brought to the garden in 1759. This modest plant is a source of clinically vital alkaloids, sixty of which have been isolated in the quest for a cure for cancer.

Return to the statue and turn towards Swan Walk. On the left, a bed of culinary and medicinal herbs has been classified into those used for dyeing, perfumery and homoeopathy. Here too you will find a Cork Oak (*Quercus suber*) and a 30-foot-high Olive tree (*Olea europaea*). The largest in the country, it bears fruit in December and is remarkably fertile for so northern a situation. Before leaving the garden spare a glance for the Pomegranate (*Punica granatum*) by the wall, left of the gate. Fruiting from July to September, it is an august member of a garden which remains an oasis of cultivation amid the busy city that has grown up around its walls.

While in Chelsea, it would be a pity to miss the gardens of the Royal Hospital. Most people know of the Hospital, if only by the familiar Chelsea Pensioner in his scarlet coat and ceremonial tricorn hat. The Chelsea Flower Show, held each May in the Hospital grounds, is an event no serious gardener should miss. Organised by the Royal Horticultural Society, the first of these 'Great Spring Shows', as they are officially known, took place in 1913.

The Hospital owns 60 acres. Through Burton's Court, north of Royal Hospital Road, runs the avenue intended to link the building to the King's Road. The King in question was Charles II, founder of the hospital for army veterans. Tradition cites Nell Gwyn, the King's mistress, as the driving force behind its establishment in 1682, but it was Sir Stephen Fox, Paymaster-General, who footed the bill for much of the work.

The gardens are open most weekdays and Sunday afternoons. Enter them via London Gate on Royal Hospital Road. On your left over 10,000 Pensioners and others are buried in the graveyard, including William Cheselden, pioneer of

modern surgery; the musicologist Dr Burney, father of Fanny, the witty novelist; and two women who, disguised as men, served as privates in Marlborough's army – one of them, Mother Ross (alias Christian Davies), died in 1739.

Ranelagh Gardens lie between the Hospital and Chelsea Bridge Road. Laid out in 1860 by John Gibson, they occupy the site of the famous Ranelagh Pleasure Gardens, fashionable in the late 18th century, which offered fireworks, masquerades and music (eight-year-old Mozart performed here when living nearby, at 180 Ebury Street). Today the 14 acres have a good collection of trees and shrubs. As well as spring flowers you may see irises, hardy perennials, roses and bedding varieties such as pansies, geraniums and polyanthus. With the formation of the Embankment in 1874, the south grounds laid out by Sir Christopher Wren lost their grandeur, though some fine planes and chestnut trees continue to flourish.

51 *American* Iris innominata *stand out boldly against the dark basaltic lava of the earliest rock garden in England, created at the Chelsea Physic Garden by Sir Joseph Banks.*

Tradescant Garden

At the junction of Lambeth Road with Lambeth Palace Road, on the south bank of the Thames, lies the Tradescant Garden. This tiny ¼-acre plot occupies the churchyard of St Mary's, a disused church rescued from neglect in 1976. It stands virtually on the doorstep of 15th-century Lambeth Palace, official residence of the Archbishop of Canterbury.

The garden belongs to the Tradescant Trust. Its namesakes are two great 17th-century plant collectors: John Tradescant (1577–1637) and his son, also John (1608–62). The father, who was possibly of Dutch extraction, worked as a gardener for Robert Cecil, 1st Earl of Salisbury, then for the Duke of Buckingham and finally for Charles I. When he died, his son succeeded him as Royal Gardener. They introduced to England such plants as the Tulip Tree, the Red Maple, the Yucca and the Red Trumpet Honeysuckle – all discovered on their travels to North Africa, Russia and America and planted in their now vanished garden at the family home in Lambeth. *Tradescantia virginiana*, the familiar Spiderwort, is named after them since they were the first to grow it in this country.

The church, too, has played a part in history: James II's second wife sheltered in St Mary's with her son one night in 1688 en route to exile in France. Five archbishops are buried inside, including the twin of General Cornwallis, leader of the British against the Americans in the War of Independence. This is also the resting place of Captain Bligh of the *Bounty* (a local resident) and, of course, of the Tradescants themselves, whose ornate tomb dominates the north-west corner of the graveyard.

The Tradescant Trust, which saved the church from demolition, has now converted it into a Garden History Museum and has transformed the church-yard into an early-17th-century garden. The Marchioness of Salisbury, whose ancestors first employed John Tradescant senior, supervised the planting of the intricate knot garden. All the species used would have been known or intro-duced by father and son. The Queen Mother opened the garden on 26 May 1983, 300 years after Elias Ashmole was buried in the church. A friend of the Tradescants, he established Oxford's Ashmolean Museum, which is based on their collection of curiosities from around the world. June is the best time to see the garden, though it is open from March to December every day except for Saturdays. A donation is welcome, since all the Trust's work is done voluntarily.

Against the east wall prospers a False Acacia (*Robinia pseudoacacia*) – a speci-men was brought back by the younger Tradescant from America in 1636; and hidden among the greenery there is a rare Plymouth Strawberry plant (*Fragaria fructu hispida*). Against the south wall you will notice a Bird Cherry (*Prunus padus*) and a Swamp Cypress (*Taxodium distichum*), more Tradescant discoveries.

The low yew hedges of the knot garden, with a striped holly (*Ilex* 'Golden King') at its centre, enclose such flowers as Heartsease (*Viola tricolor*), Red-Leaved Plantain (*Plantago major rubrifolia*), Cuckoo Flower (*Cardamine pratensis*), yellow Dusty Miller (*Primula auricula*) and the Christmas Rose (*Helleborus niger*), which blooms in January and February.

Among the more unusual species are a towering 9-foot-high Monkshood (*Aconitum napellus*), which is highly poisonous, Wild Bergamot (*Monarda fistulosa*), Red Baneberry (*Actaea rubra*) and the luscious Cardinal Flower (*Lobelia cardin-alis*), so called because when it was first presented to Charles I's wife, she compared it to a cardinal's scarlet stocking.

Many of the plants are gifts: Kew has supplied Spotted Deadnettles (*Lamium maculatum*) and Rust-Coloured Foxgloves (*Digitalis ferruginea*); Chelsea Physic Garden has sent the fragrant Mignonette, the Mandrake and Pomegranate. Plants are also dispatched from America; and through the Trust's sponsored exchange visits for horticulturalists, the Tradescants' traditions of exploration and research are furthered on both sides of the Atlantic.

LORD
HOLLAND
BORN
MDCCLXXIII
DIED
MDCCCL

Gardens for the Gardenless

Cannizaro Park

So few people know Cannizaro Park. Situated on the east side of Wimbledon Common, it combines the formality of its Dutch sunken garden with the wild romanticism of towering trees and grassy slopes.

The Georgian house around which it extends was rebuilt after a fire in 1900. It was home first to Thomas Walker, Commissioner of Customs, who lived here from 1744 to 1748. Subsequent tenants included Henry Dundas, Viscount Melville, who planted the giant beeches in Lady Jane's Wood (to the south) in honour of his wife. William Pitt the Younger, his close friend, treated the mansion as a second home, and somewhere here grows a tree with his name carved into the bark. Another owner was the Duke of Cannizaro. This impoverished Sicilian nobleman evidently found the English climate a strain (or was his wife the problem?) for he fled back to Italy, his desperate spouse in hot pursuit. In the late 19th century Lord Tennyson, Oscar Wilde and Henry James, among many other celebrities, came to parties held here by the society hostess Mrs Schuster. The shipping magnate Edward K. Wilson was the last private owner. His daughter sold the house and grounds to the local authority in 1948 and today (1986) the future of the mansion hangs in the balance. Wimbledon residents want it to stay open as an exhibition venue; the council is determined to sell it as office space.

Herbaceous beds border the driveway which leads to the garden, in true Victorian fashion. Strange chatterings of captive birds come from a modern aviary ahead, a white-painted miniature version of Pisa Cathedral. Spreading behind the house are 6 acres of rolling lawns and woods, with fine views across Surrey, which include the distant spire of Leatherhead Church. Against the rear wall of the house thrives a Chinese Evergreen Magnolia (*Magnolia delavayi*), which produces luxurious cream flowers in early summer, while near to the aviary grow Japanese Red Maples, an uncommon Black Gum (*Nyssa sylvatica*) – distinguished by its grey bark – and along the path leading off from the aviary, at right angles to the drive, a 30-foot-high Big-Leaf Storax (*Styrax obassia*), uncommon in England. If you go right of the big beech tree and duck under the group of large hollies, there against the boundary wall you will find the moss-covered tombstones of Susie, Button, Spookie and other Wilson pets.

Follow the path; as it swings to the left you can walk through a large break in the wall to a triangular section of garden, set slightly apart. This belonged to The Keir, a house no longer standing. Straight ahead, hugging the south-facing wall, are exotic Pomegranate, Yellow Kowhai (*Sophora tetraptera*) and *Ribes*

52 *Henry Richard Fox, 3rd Baron Holland and owner of Holland House, as portrayed by G.F. Watts (a protégé of Holland's) and Edgar Boehm, 1869–70. The statue is at the end of Rose Walk in Holland Park (see pp. 86–9), overlooking the pond; behind it lies dense woodland. Walter Scott wrote of Holland Park's 'air of deep seclusion which is spread around the domain' – an atmosphere that can still occasionally be felt even though Holland Park, like many of London's once-private aristocratic preserves, is now a much-appreciated 'garden for the gardenless'.*

speciosum, which has red fuchsia-like blooms. The small 19th-century Gothic priest's-house is all that remains of a chapel erected by The Keir's Catholic owner. Keeping the house on your right, you pass by a circular rose-bed, near which is the unusual Hedgehog Holly (*Ilex ferox*). Beyond, and beneath an ancient Mulberry tree, is a bust of Haile Selassie. Horse Chestnuts line the east–west path, which culminates in a statue of 'Little Diana', who is cradling a faun. Birches and deliciously scented Balsam Poplars lead south towards a pond. The lawn in front of the house sports an impressive 70-foot Scarlet Oak (*Quercus coccinea*) and an unusual Turner's Oak.

The woodland gardens dominate the southern part of Cannizaro and lie beyond the brick wall enclosing what was the kitchen garden. Follow the wall round to the left and take the path which goes between it and the small stream. On the banks, primulas, lilies and ferns flourish, and azaleas and rhododendrons are gloriously rampant. Walking beneath the poplars with the woodland garden on your left, cross the small stone bridge and follow the path through the woods. Here and there sudden explosions of colour break up the dense green of the undergrowth. Two paths break away to the left. Take the second, and then a path leading off to the right, opposite a tall carbuncled tree. Here some steep steps lead through azaleas which have been laced into a tunnel up to an observation point. Through a clearing in the trees you can see the dell below, crammed with blossom in May. The surrounding woodland is mainly oak, though there are some impressive hollies forming a backdrop to ornamental plants. At the edge of the wood nearest the house you will find a mature potent-

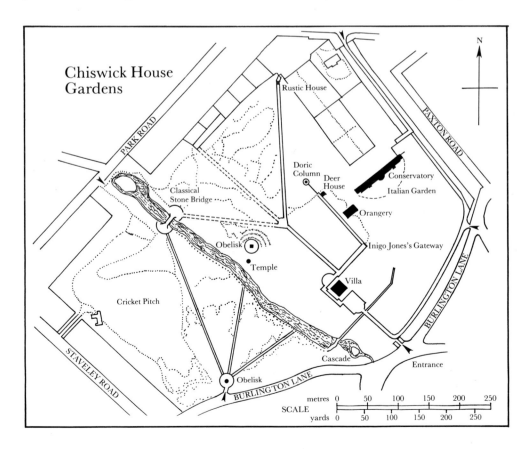

53 *In the neo-classical garden of Chiswick House, 18th-century sphinxes and urns line the avenue leading from the house to an exedra formed by statues of eminent Romans. The path is flanked by cedars and cypresses.*

OVERLEAF
54 *The garden front of Chiswick House, seen through cypress trees. Originally the extension to a Jacobean house (since demolished) it was designed as a summer villa where its first owner, Lord Burlington, could entertain his friends – one of whom, the poet Alexander Pope, described it as 'the finest thing this glorious sun has shined upon'.*

smelling Sassafras tree. Early American settlers used the young growths in tea to combat scurvy. Here, too, is the rare and refined Russian Birch (*Betula ermanii*), which has a dull pinky bark.

At the southern end, near Chester Road, is the heather garden. The brightest coloured plants are grouped by the Belvedere, a viewing terrace decorated with miniature obelisks and columns crowned with carved arrangements of fruit.

Before leaving Wimbledon, spare some time for the Common. During the 19th century the Lords of the Manor wanted to build on it, but the Commons Preservation Society fought the attempt and fortunately won.

Chiswick House

If you walk in the grounds of Chiswick House you may meet the strange little lady who tells visitors that there is a spell on the place. She could be right, for the gardens have the kind of magic associated with secret paths, follies and doors leading nowhere.

A Jacobean mansion which stood on this land passed to the Earl of Burlington in 1682. Richard Boyle, the 3rd Earl (1695–1753) and a patron of the arts, was responsible for the present house and gardens (**54**). Travels in Italy had fostered a love of Palladian architecture which led him to design a villa based on Palladio's Villa Rotonda, near Vicenza. This new house survived the older mansion, which was demolished in 1788, but not everyone admired it. The caustic Lord Hervey, for instance, described Chiswick House as 'too small to inhabit and too large to hang on a watch-chain'.

Inspired too by Italian countryside and the landscape paintings of Claude and Poussin, Burlington employed Charles Bridgeman and William Kent to create a garden in the 'natural style' of which they were the leading exponents. Burlington's circle, which included the poet Alexander Pope, thought the Dutch topiary and knot gardens then in fashion too contrived, yet to us Kent's designs seem scarcely more natural. His idealised vision of the country had no visible boundaries but was decorated with temples and grottoes chanced upon near serpentine rivers or set on small hills. This element of surprise was carefully orchestrated. There were also statues of Roman senators (with whom aristocrats like Burlington could identify), groves, glades and apparently random clumps of trees. Many of these elements were brought to Chiswick. Walking here was to be an exercise that drew upon the spectator's cultural, philosophical and artistic sensibilities.

The avenues planted by Kent lay along the axes of the formal garden already in existence, and therefore the design remained symmetrical. Three narrow *allées* radiated from the north front of the house, but only one survives. Because Burlington wanted the park to seem as large as possible, the hedges that bordered the *allées* were grown high and the garden buildings upon which they converged were miniatures, creating clever false perspectives.

After Burlington's death, Chiswick House passed to the Dukes of Devonshire and the later 18th century saw the garden design softened. The 5th Duke of Devonshire kept American deer in the grounds; they were so savage that his son would not venture out unless armed with a sword. This same young man, as the 6th Duke, later installed a menagerie, including a kangaroo and an elephant. The Italian Garden to the east of the house was laid out at this time. In 1928 the house, having temporarily served as a lunatic asylum, was presented to the nation, and Hounslow Council took charge of the grounds.

An avenue flanked by Kent's double row of Lebanon Cedars and limes runs straight towards the villa from the main entrance, in Burlington Lane, south of the house (see map). Ancient English Oaks also grow in this area. The broad path continues on the north side of the building and is embellished with urns and sphinxes (**53**). It leads to a group of niches cut into myrtle and containing statues of Caesar, Pompey and Cicero dug up from Hadrian's Villa in Tivoli.

The surviving original *allée* runs north and culminates in the Rustic House, which has niches for statuary. Near here flourishes a Japanese Big-Leaf Magnolia (*Magnolia hypoleuca*) and to the west, by a small clearing, grows a group of Sweet Chestnuts, planted in the early 18th century and some of the oldest trees in the park. A gateway of the 1620s designed by Inigo Jones stands east of the villa; it was moved here in 1736 from Beaufort House, Chelsea, when Sir Hans Sloane, Burlington's physician, knowing of his intense admiration for Jones, bequeathed it to him.

The 19th-century Italian Garden was conceived for the 6th Duke of Devonshire by Lewis Kennedy and was based on designs made for Napoleon's Empress Josephine. There is a proposal to refurbish it with authentic plants. A Maidenhair Tree (*Ginkgo biloba*) thrives here and the conservatory, designed *c.* 1813 by Samuel Ware and now protecting a fine camellia collection, acts as a focal point.

Slightly west of these gardens is the Deer House, on the edge of the ha-ha, and a Doric column formerly topped by a copy of the Venus de Medici. An Ionic temple, an obelisk rising out of a pond, and a turf amphitheatre form a

55 *The beautiful bridge over the canal in the gardens of Chiswick House was designed by James Wyatt and built in 1788, replacing a wooden original. It is decorated with urns and reliefs of cherubs.*

dramatic group in the centre of the grounds. By the railings stands a monument to 'faithful Lill', an Italian greyhound. The canal, 2,000 feet long and 60 feet wide, is part of Kent's design. Towards the northern end is James Wyatt's ornate classical stone bridge of 1788 (**55**). At the opposite end is a rustic wooden one. Along the banks are beds of *Cornus alba*, Pampas Grass (*Cortaderia*), Purple Loosestrife (*Lythrum salicaria*), Meadowsweet (*Filipendula ulmaria*) and Hostas – but all this could change if the council adopts the refurbishment programme.

Running south from the stone bridge, on the western shore of the canal, is another avenue, one of three which strike away from an obelisk in the opposite corner of the park. This obelisk incorporates a Roman tombstone of the 2nd century AD showing a couple with a child. On the west of the path a fine Narrow Leafed Ash (*Fraxinus angustifolia*), almost 85 feet high, stands near the cricket pitch. The trees in the south are oak, beech, ash, chestnut, hornbeam, and sycamore, although near to the Cascade (a two-storeyed structure which once had an engine that raised the water and caused it to fall back down into the canal) grows a more unusual Tulip Tree (*Liriodendron tulipifera*). Outside the grounds, the A4's speeding traffic has marooned Hogarth's House, once the artist's country home and now a charming museum which is well worth a visit.

Gunnersbury Park

The two houses of Gunnersbury Park sit so close together they almost brush walls. Built in the 19th century, there is something feminine in their demure

appearance, and it is an interesting coincidence that many women have been attracted to this estate. The first owner was probably Gunhilda, a daughter of Canute, the 11th-century king. Three hundred years later, Alice Perrers, Edward III's mistress, ruled the roost here. The medieval manor was razed in the 17th century when Sir John Maynard, a Member of Parliament, commissioned John Webb to design him a Palladian-style villa. Later, in the 1760s, came the headstrong Princess Amelia, favourite daughter of George II. Having quit her home in Richmond (see p. 47), she spent her summers in Gunnersbury.

Webb's villa was demolished in the 1800s when the land was divided and sold. Alexander Copland put up Gunnersbury Park House (the larger mansion), later home to the Rothschilds and now containing a local history museum, open in the afternoons. Gunnersbury House (the smaller mansion) was built for either Stephen Cosser or Major Alexander Morrison but was joined to the Rothschilds' estate in 1889. Since 1926 the public has had access to the park, for which Hounslow and Ealing Councils are jointly responsible.

The main gates are on Pope's Lane, Ealing. Follow the drive around to the right, to the café, and then past the fine dahlia bed to the temple (**56**), designed for Amelia by Sir William Chambers. Classical plaster figures would once have occupied its now empty niches. The original two storeys were reduced to one in the 19th century, when it possibly served as a synagogue for the Rothschilds.

56 *The little 18th-century temple which overlooks the round boating pond in Gunnersbury Park probably dates from the time when Princess Amelia (1710–86) used to spend her summers in the villa that stood in the park. Thought to have been designed by Sir William Chambers, the temple was originally an ornamental dairy.*

On the other side of the modest boating pond stretches a herbaceous bed garbed in summer with fuchsias, petunias, cornflowers and Busy Lizzies. To the west are the nurseries, while east of both houses is the sadly neglected Gothic bath-house, which dates from the 18th century, when outdoor bathing was fashionable. Here, too, is the 'Quiet Garden', which should provoke reflection, but you cannot help noticing instead the traffic winging by on Gunnersbury Avenue on the other side of the wall. The stables are screened by sham Gothic ruins of the 19th century, and east of this group but south of the larger mansion is Sydney Smirke's lovely orangery, abandoned for many years now.

Also in a bad way is the ruined Boat House Folly (once a pottery kiln) in the south-west of the park. The Potomac fishing pond (said to be named after the popular phrase 'all quiet on the Potomac', coined during the American Civil War) was created from an old clay pit. A Strawberry Tree (*Arbutus unedo*) and Pillar Apples (*Malus tschonoskii*) grow nearby, and some noble indigenous trees in this southern area testify to the former beauty of the estate before the cricket and football pitches took over.

Ham House

The stretch of river between Richmond and Teddington is remarkably rural; the aspect of meadows and trees can have changed little since the 17th century. In the midst of this stand Ham House and its cultivated formal gardens, which seem all the more highly wrought for the wildness of their setting.

The house was built in 1610 for Sir Thomas Vavasour, Knight Marshal of James I. At the time it conformed to a traditional Jacobean H-plan design. Over the years both interior and exterior were altered. William Murray, who acquired the property in 1630, had as a child been Charles I's whipping boy, literally taking a thrashing on behalf of the Prince when the young Charles misbehaved. For his pains, Murray was made the Earl of Dysart. His daughter Elizabeth, an ambitious and able woman, was responsible for most of the modifications to the house. After the death of her first husband, she took a lover – Oliver Cromwell, Lord Protector of England. Made Countess of Dysart in her own right, in 1669 she married John Maitland, Duke of Lauderdale, who was promoted to High Commissioner for Scotland, but was loathed by the Scots, whom he milked of money to furnish Ham House.

You can reach Ham by the no. 65 bus from Richmond, which passes a pedestrian entrance on Petersham Road. If you are travelling by car, leave Petersham Road via Sandy Lane and turn off into Ham Street. There is a free car park by the river. The gardens are open every day except for Monday and some public holidays and belong, with the house, to the National Trust. Pass down the avenue of limes which replaced the dying elms in 1950. The entrance gate was designed in 1671 by Sir William Bruce, Elizabeth's cousin, and is painted in the original blue and gold. In the 17th century the house was approached by avenues leading from Petersham to the east and Ham to the south, as the position of the gates on the other side of the building suggests; a third avenue, leading from the front entrance to a landing stage on the riverside, was swept away when the north court was restyled *c.* 1799. Thirty-eight busts were inserted into ovals on the three walls which enclosed this front courtyard. Of these Roman emperors and ladies, twenty-two are still in their original positions but sixteen were removed when the forecourt wall was replaced by a

gravel walk, and repositioned in the ovals on the front of the house. The pineapples along the railings also date from 1799, as does the statue of a reclining Father Thames.

The Principal Garden, or Cherry Garden, is to the east of the house. Beautifully formal, it has arbours of pleached hornbeam and yew hedges. In the centre, geometric beds are bordered by hedges and miniature obelisks of Dwarf Box (*Buxus sempervirens suffruticosa*). In the beds are Cotton Lavender plants (*Santolina chamaecyparissus*), which form an unusual undulating surface.

Behind the house on the south side the National Trust has re-created the grounds as they would have been in the early 1670s, using suitable plants. You leave the high terrace for a set of eight neat squares of lawn divided by gravel paths. The original shingle was dug from the Pen Ponds, Richmond Park. Ahead spreads the Wilderness – trees and hedges laid out in a formal *patte d'oie* (goosefoot) pattern. Hornbeam hedges and Field Maples branch away from a circular clearing with grassy walks between. The central avenue continues the line of its southern counterpart, which heads for Ham. The eight wooden chairs in the clearing are replicas of those first introduced to the garden. Poplars and hollies alternate along the southern wall.

To the west of the house, the former kitchen garden is now devoted to roses (**57**). The holly walk running east–west beyond the lawn focuses on a 17th-century statue of Bacchus anxiously scrutinising a bunch of grapes. In the middle of the lawn rises the oldest tree in the grounds, an oak, while on either side roses fill the beds and clamber across the aged brick walls.

The stables, now privately owned, lie behind the brick orangery. This wisteria-clad building serves as a tea pavilion, and in spring and summer tables are put outside. Near to the building, protected by railings, spread an unusual Christ's Thorn Tree (*Paliurus spina-christi*) and a Judas Tree (*Cercis silaquastrum*).

When you leave the grounds take a walk along the towpath. Looking east you see Richmond Hill, while Petersham Meadows, home of a little working farm and herd of cows, brush the riverbank. In fine weather look among the tussocks for a discreet sign telling you to wave for the ferry. If you were thinking of visiting Marble Hill House on the opposite shore (see pp. 93–5), why not cross the Thames this way, as people have done for centuries?

The Hill Gardens and Golders Hill Park

You feel you could meet a distraught Victorian heroine or a pair of tragic lovers in London's most secret garden, The Hill. Its dramatic pergola, raised high above the ground, has white pillars entangled in creepers, wisteria and climbing roses, providing the combination of profusion and decay so appealing to true romantics.

The Hill Gardens form part of Hampstead Heath, and once belonged to the adjoining house, now a private hospital. The gardens are the creation of an earlier owner of the house, Lord Leverhulme. This Edwardian patron of the arts employed the architect Thomas H. Mawson to create a landscape of colonnades, pavilions, stone paths, pools and the pergola. To do this he used earth excavated during the construction at the beginning of this century of the nearby Northern Line underground.

Enter the grounds from Inverforth Close, off North End Way in Hampstead. High brick walls reinforce the sense of privacy. Before you spreads a formal garden with a rectangular pool, sets of steps on three sides and, on the fourth, a lawn gently sloping south. In winter the dense shrubs are brightened by the addition of cotoneaster and holly berries, while in spring and summer the paths are crowded with rhododendrons and hydrangeas. Climb the steps to the raised pergola on the east side. The house lies to the north, in its own private garden. Peer over the wrought-iron bays or through the columns at the cloistered arches below the walkway and at nature gone mad in the former kitchen garden below.

For a complete contrast wander back across the equally untamed Heath to Golders Hill Park, which adjoins The Hill on its west side. Here you are back in civilisation. From gently undulating lawns you have, on a clear day, a view of the Harrow hills. Pink flamingos adorn a small lake which is trimmed by brilliantly coloured herbaceous beds, while at the southern end of the park a small domestic zoo of deer, cockerels, rabbits and storks is reminiscent of the menageries so common in 18th-century parklands and gardens.

Holland Park

It seems extraordinary that you can walk in a wood so close to the centre of London. Holland Park's 55 acres of woodland and formal gardens are a haven for anyone interested in rare trees or simply seeking to escape from frantic Kensington High Street.

Cope's Castle was built on this land in 1607 for Sir Walter Cope, Chancellor of the Exchequer. The house passed to Henry Rich, Earl of Holland, who gave

58 *Holland House is a Jacobean mansion begun in 1605 for Sir Walter Cope (who was Keeper of Hyde Park). It is named after his son-in-law, the 1st Earl of Holland. The house was a meeting-place for disgruntled Parliamentarians during Charles I's reign; in the 18th and 19th centuries it was the venue of a distinguished artistic and political salon. The loggias that run along the centre and the wings of the house were fashionable innovations in early 17th-century architecture.*

59 *Holland House's 18th century ice-house is now used largely for craft exhibitions. Ice-houses were introduced into England by Charles II's gardener, Mr Rose, in 1660, in imitation of those at Versailles, where the King had spent much of his exile. They were used for keeping food cold, so that even in warm weather it was possible to enjoy delicious ices.*

the property its name. Inigo Jones added two further wings to the building and with the help of the sculptor Nicholas Stone designed the gateway east of the Court Theatre. Wavering between the Roundheads and Cavaliers, Rich backed the latter and lost his head as a result, leaving his property temporarily in the hands of the opposition. With the Restoration of 1660 it was retrieved by Lady Isabel Holland.

In the early 19th century Holland House became a celebrated centre for the talented and influential. Henry Richard Fox, the 3rd Baron, and a Whig Member of Parliament, entertained Talleyrand, Lord Byron and Charles Dickens here. Napoleon was also a family friend and donated to the garden a bronze bust of himself. This has disappeared, but a statue of the Baron (**52**) can still be seen in the northern part of the park.

The 4th Baron Holland, with whom the title expired, spent much time abroad but in 1850 added to the grounds an orangery (now an exhibition venue) and converted the 17th-century stables into a garden ballroom (now the Belvedere restaurant). World War II's bombs virtually destroyed the house, sparing only the east wing (**58**), which since 1959 has been a Youth Hostel.

Strolling up tree-lined Holland Walk from the Kensington Gate you pass the Commonwealth Institute and then the hostel on your left. Head north towards Holland Park Gate. In a collection of trees on the left, level with the pond, grows a rare Himalayan Birch (*Betula utilis*), distinguished by its silvery bark. Clustered near the gate itself are a 150-year-old Wild Pear (*Pyrus communis*) and a scarce Violet Willow (*Salix daphnoides*). Taking Chestnut Walk, which leads south-west

off Holland Walk, you will come across the exquisite Snowdrop Tree (*Halesia monticola*), which blooms in May.

In the north-west corner of the park, by the North Abbotsbury Road entrance, lies the D-shaped garden (with a section of brick wall), once part of the kitchen garden. Here is the lone survivor of some cedars planted in 1798. Lime Tree Walk, dating from 1876, runs east at a 45° angle to Chestnut Walk. Follow it back across the park towards the little pond presided over by the statue of the 3rd Lord Holland, sculpted by G. F. Watts and J. E. Boehm. Behind him note the uncommon Pin Oak (*Quercus palustris*).

Purple willowherb and white convolvulus wax wild in the undergrowth and the fenced areas are home to a tribe of hens, rabbits and squirrels. Sometimes you can spot peacocks roosting in the trees, their bright tails hanging down like exotic foliage. South of the pond, Rose Walk, which boasts a very rare Pyrenean Oak (*Quercus pyrenaica*) bearing July catkins, leads to the North Lawn. Here there is a Chinese Sweet Gum (*Liquidambar formosana*) and a Twisted Ash (*Fraxinus elonza*) – both extremely rare.

To the west, the Yucca Lawn is patrolled by gorgeous silver pheasants, rheas, cranes and guinea-fowl. Uncommon trees include the very rare Variegated London Plane (*Platanus* x *acerifolia* 'Suttneri') and the Single-Leafed Ash (*Fraxinus excelsior* 'Diversifolia'). A terrace runs south of this lawn, spreading in front of the house, hostel and formal garden, whose low hedges and geometric flower-beds were laid out in 1812. This garden is floodlit at night and stays open until 12pm, which is marvellous for those who like strolling among flowers before going to bed. The Napoleonic Gardens, to the west, are so called because the Emperor's bust stood here. Rogers's Seat, tucked into a wall, in the fireplace of the original stable building, is named after the poet Samuel Rogers, a friend

60 *Kenwood House, a plain early-17th-century mansion enlarged and beautified by Robert Adam in the 18th century, presides majestically over the grand sweep of its grounds. Bequeathed to the nation in 1927 by Lord Iveagh, it houses a great art collection.*

of Lord Holland. The Belvedere restaurant and orangery lie to the south, with the pretty Iris Garden nestling between. It was here in 1804 that the first dahlias were cultivated in England. On one side of the orangery the former ice-house (**59**) accommodates occasional exhibitions, while on the other a Rose Garden looks splendid in June. Just behind Holland House is the outdoor Court Theatre, where you can enjoy a play or a concert on a warm summer evening.

Kenwood and Hampstead Heath

Hampstead Heath is like a massive park, of which the grounds of Kenwood House are but a small part. Locals are fiercely possessive about *their* heath, and since the 1830s have valiantly fought off any attempted plunder by would-be developers. The area is too sprawling to cover on a short visit, but it does subdivide into manageable portions.

To the south-east spread Parliament Hill Fields. The hill is said (without much foundation) to be named after Parliamentary elections once held here. Equally tenuous is the idea that it has something to do with the Gunpowder Plot (1605), whose authors are supposed to have congregated here to get a good view of the Houses of Parliament going up in smoke. The hill is 320 feet high and from the top you can spot many London landmarks and, on a clear day, parts of Kent. To the north, a second hill, known as the Tumulus, was possibly an ancient burial site (it is romantically known as 'Boadicea's Grave'). The six Highgate Ponds are strung like a necklace along the north-east boundary. In one men can swim; in another women; and everyone can take a dip together in one of the Hampstead Ponds, to the south-west.

In the main part of the Heath you can imagine yourself in the heart of the

OVERLEAF
61 *The lake and sham bridge at Kenwood, with the dense South Wood in the background, are like a stage set for a Shakespeare play. On June and August evenings they form a backdrop to open-air symphony concerts. The 'bridge' was designed to act as an eye-catcher from Kenwood House.*

62 *The primary colours of the fair draw people to Hampstead Heath at Easter, Whitsun and during the summer.*

country. In the 18th century the discovery of mineral springs made Hampstead (then a village) fashionable, and long after its medicinal reputation waned it remained an exclusive place to live. Perhaps this fuelled the greed of the absentee Lord of the Manor, Sir Thomas Maryon Wilson, who in 1829 tried to supply the demand for building land with slivers from the Heath. A battle began between him and the local residents which lasted until his death in the 1870s. Despite an Act of 1866 preventing the enclosure of common land within a 14-mile radius of Charing Cross, Wilson started to build. His men wrenched up undergrowth and planted ornamental trees for residential streets. He also sold off thousands of tons of the Heath's sand, leaving ugly scars on the surface. Gorse seed was scattered later to cover these blemishes, which accounts for the appearance of the landscape today. Fortunately on Wilson's death his brother agreed to sell the land to public authorities at an affordable price so that the Heath could stay open.

The East Heath's elms, oaks and Horse Chestnuts surround the Vale of Health, where D. H. Lawrence lived for a time, with Katherine Mansfield a near neighbour in East Heath Road. To the south of East Heath are the magnificent limes of Boundary Path – a pleasant avenue to walk in. Apart from Golders Hill and the Hill Gardens (see pp. 85–6) the most famous and highest landmark is Jack Straw's Castle, north of Whitestone Pond on North End Way, a tavern dating from the 18th century and favoured by Charles Dickens. On the same side of the road are the birch, oak, ash, hawthorns and chestnuts of the densely wooded West Heath. Take a stroll from Whitestone Pond down Judge's Walk, where, according to popular belief, the court sessions were held in times of plague. The Sandy Heath and Heath Extension lie in the triangle between North End Way and Spaniards Road, on the other side of which extend the grounds of Kenwood (Caen Wood) House (**60**).

Although there were several owners in the 18th century, this mansion is most closely associated with William Murray, 1st Earl of Mansfield, who was Attorney General and Lord Chief Justice to George III. He employed Robert Adam to improve the original early-17th-century house in 1767. Adam added another story and a library to balance the existing orangery so that the south front would be symmetrical. Further wings were built in the 1790s at the instigation of the 2nd Earl.

The landscaping of the grounds was mainly the work of Murray, who planted the cedars on the lawn with his own hands. The lake and sham bridge (**61**) probably date from his time. The 2nd Earl may well have sought advice from the gardener Humphry Repton, for the grounds bear the hallmark of that famous landscape designer: an emphasis on lawns and flowers near the home. The house stood empty for long periods in the 19th century but was rented for seven years in the early 20th by Michael, Grand Duke of Russia. In 1925 Lord Iveagh bought the estate and a few years later he bequeathed it to the nation.

The main gates to the grounds are on Hampstead Lane and two drives meander through the thick North Wood towards the house. You have a delightful feeling of anticipation, for you get no glimpse of the building until you are more or less upon it. Inside you can admire the exquisite Adam interiors and the famous collection of paintings by Gainsborough, Reynolds, Vermeer and many others.

Running back towards Hampstead from the orangery is an avenue of limes which has replaced one where, according to tradition, Alexander Pope liked to wander and compose verse. At the back of the house the land sweeps towards woods (**1**) and the concert lake. On summer evenings prestigious orchestras perform, their music wafting across the water. Some of the audience of 8,000 or so pay to sit in deckchairs by the lake's edge; others for a smaller fee prefer to loll on the grass with a picnic. Around the lake are Holm Oaks and Sweet Chestnuts while in the South Wood, behind, grow some of the finest beeches in England, rivalled only by the thick clumps of rhododendrons all around.

Marble Hill, Orleans House and York House

Extensive lawns punctuated by clumps of trees surround the fine Palladian villa at Marble Hill, Twickenham, and form an outstanding example of an 18th-century landscaped park.

This riverside estate was acquired piecemeal by Lord Ilay on behalf of Henrietta Howard, mistress to the future George II and later Countess of Suffolk. Wooed for her wit and intelligence rather than for her beauty, Henrietta was given an allowance by George so that she could build Marble Hill. Roger Morris designed the chastely beautiful villa (**63**) with advice from Lord Herbert, and it was completed *c.* 1729. The grounds meanwhile were taken in hand by Charles Bridgeman, who went on to be Royal Gardener to both George I and George II. Bridgeman favoured an informal style of gardens. It was he who introduced into England the *fosse* or ha-ha, a sunken ditch that provided a boundary without interfering with the view. Helping him with the planning was Henrietta's good friend the poet Alexander Pope, a Twickenham

resident. A second regular visitor was Jonathan Swift who, acknowledging Pope as 'the contriver of the gardens' and 'Lord Herbert [as] the architect', described his own role as 'chief butler and keeper of the ice-house'. The poet and playwright John Gay inhabited a little cottage (no longer standing) adjacent to the house, and Horace Walpole, another neighbour, encouraged the Countess to construct a 'Gothic priory' in her garden, but it was pulled down on her death.

Swift was so fond of the estate that he wrote a poem entitled 'A Pastoral Dialogue between Richmond Lodge and Marble Hill' (1727). In it he predicted a terrible fate for the pretty villa:

> Some South Sea broker from the city,
> Will purchase me, the more's the pity,
> Lay all my fine plantations waste,
> To fit them to his vulgar taste;

And at the turn of the century this very nearly was the case. The shipping magnate William Cunard acquired the property, and, to the horror of those who lived nearby, began to develop the grounds for housing. Strangely enough what caused the uproar was not so much that the villa would be destroyed and the park carved up by roads but that the view of uninterrupted green from Richmond Hill would be ruined. Fortunately Cunard's 'vulgar taste' was frustrated when the local councils got together and decided to purchase the estate. Marble Hill has thus been a park since 1903; the beautifully maintained house was first opened to the public in 1967.

The main gates to Marble Hill are on the Richmond Road, Twickenham. Car-drivers can leave their vehicles in the free car park in the grounds. There

63 *Marble Hill House was built 1724–9; the first owner of this exquisite villa was Henrietta Howard, George II's mistress. A later inhabitant was Maria Fitzherbert, a twice-widowed Catholic who clandestinely – and illegally – married the Prince Regent, later George IV. Marble Hill's gardens were laid out by Charles Bridgeman, with advice from Alexander Pope.*

are some fine trees to be seen, including the tallest Lombardy Poplars (*Populus italica*) in Britain – 120 feet high – and, by the southern, river exit, a Black Walnut (*Juglans nigra*) surrounded by railings, 72 feet high and as old as the house. Other trees include yew, willow, chestnut, oak and cedar.

Behind the villa, to the east, is a grotto. (A smaller companion recorded in 1767 has vanished.) Grottoes, artificial caves providing a cool retreat in hot weather, were a popular feature of 18th-century gardens. Inside, alcoves held busts and the walls and ceilings were clad with pebbles or shells; sometimes they even boasted springs or a fountain. This one was rediscovered in 1941 when a falling elm caved in the roof; it was then forgotten once more, but was stumbled on again in 1983. It is now about 6 feet below present ground level but its restorers hope to reconstruct the façade and interior exactly as they once were. North-west of the villa, Swift's ice-house is totally buried in the thickets of the bird sanctuary. The converted 19th-century stable block nearby offers refreshments.

Leaving by the western gate and turning left down narrow Orleans Road, you come to an archway in a brick wall on your right. Orleans House Gallery is here, open in the afternoons. Unfortunately the 18th-century house once on this site did not have its neighbour's luck and in 1926 all but a small part was demolished by a gravel merchant who wanted to dig the land. The Octagon (**64**), or Garden Room, survives; it was created later than the rest of the house, in 1720, in honour of a visit by Caroline of Ansbach, George II's queen. The surrounding

64 *This beautiful octagon, now an art gallery, is all that survives of 18th-century Orleans House. It was designed c. 1720 by James Gibbs and used as a garden room; a reception was given here to welcome to England Caroline of Ansbach, George II's queen and a friend of the house's owner, James Johnson. The interior is sumptuously decorated with plasterwork by the famous Italian plasterers Artari and Bagutti.*

gardens had a reputation for their fruit and in the 17th century Queen Anne, then Princess of Denmark, dined off cherries from the grounds.

The house is named after another famous resident, Louis Philippe, Duc d'Orléans, who settled here in the early 1800s. In 1882 Cunard, the owner of Marble Hill, bought Orleans House and his wife lived on here after his death. In 1927 Mrs Ionides bought the Octagon and in 1962 she left it to the nation as a gallery, together with her own collection of topographical paintings.

The remains of the wooded grounds are enchanting. Wild flowers such as mallow, docks, deadnettles, bluebells, willowherb, cow parsley and violets grow here, as well as daffodils and crocuses. The trees range from the stolid – sycamore and Horse Chestnut – to the ornamental – Plum and Cherry. Shrubs include yellow Laburnum, purple Buddleia and pure white Snowberry.

From these dappled grounds, head west towards Twickenham town centre, along Richmond Road or via Riverside, the road running parallel with the river, to York House. Designed in the early 17th century, it belonged to the Earl of Clarendon, whose daughter Anne married the Duke of York, Charles II's unpopular brother. Clarendon's grand-daughters, Mary and Anne, were both to be Queens of England. In 1864 the house was sold to the Duc d'Aumale for his nephew the Comte de Paris, a grandson of King Louis Philippe. The last private owner was a wealthy Parsee industrialist, Sir Ratan Tata. The building has been municipal offices since 1926.

The garden has changed a good deal since the time of its original tenants. A Dutch garden has given way to a car park and a kitchen garden has been converted into tennis courts. Nevertheless, between the house and river there remains a lovely south front with a sunken lawn introduced by Sir Ratan, bordered by flower-beds. An arched stone bridge rises high above a lane and links the lawn with the riverside gardens. These are divided into three separate areas: that on the extreme right is marked out by its 'naked ladies'. These Italian statues were brought here to screen an ugly warehouse which has since gone. An electrical device once operated a fountain. Made out of Portland Stone, these nymphs are subject to frequent vandalism and graffiti, yet – although they might seem more at home under the sunny skies of the Mediterranean – they appear to be putting on a brave face, dangling their beautiful white limbs above chilly water. The balustraded terrace, along the back of the garden, overlooks the river and Eel Pie Island, where Victorian day-trippers used to come and eat that curiously English dish.

Osterley Park

'There is nowhere so near London where one can stand and look across fields used for agriculture, and where real horses graze and there are large elms, natural thickets and real weeds, and see proper country and avoid that sense of municipal attention which one gets even in better known spaces in London . . .' Sir John Betjeman was writing of Osterley Park in a letter of 1963 registering protest against a proposed plan to build a multinational conference centre in the grounds, with an hotel and staff flats. Fortunately a public inquiry scotched this vile scheme, but not the M4 motorway, which, a few years later, tore the parkland roughly in half. The northern part is now leased to tenant farmers as pasture; the southern area remains with the house; both have belonged to the National Trust since 1949. Despite all this, the house and gardens retain their

65 *Osterley Park was planted by the Child family in the 18th century; 3,000 trees were introduced in 1780 alone. Most were beech, intended for both ornamental and commercial purposes. The park is on the site of woods notorious throughout the Middle Ages for outlaws, and of a fort that protected convoys travelling between London and Windsor.*

quiet dignity, and walking in the grounds is much like walking in a beautifully maintained private estate.

Sir Thomas Gresham, founder of the Royal Exchange and Chancellor of the Exchequer to Elizabeth I, built the red-brick mansion. The year after its completion in 1578 Elizabeth paid him a visit. She commented, perhaps idly, that the court would look better divided by a wall. That night as she slept Gresham summoned workmen from London and by morning a partition had been raised. The estate passed to the Childs, a banking family, at the start of the 18th century. Sir Francis Child, and then his brother Robert, carried out substantial modernising work, employing Robert Adam as architect. Preserving the original plan, he encased the building in new walls in a classical style. The Elizabethan gardens were swept away and replaced by informal parkland designed by Robert Child's wife and her steward, Mr Bunce. Straight-lined avenues of trees were laid out towards the mansion, and they still exist, as does the walled vegetable garden, north of the house, but the Wilderness, west of it, has gone. Mrs Child converted ponds into three lakes curving around the house, and across the northern one Robert Adam strung a bridge which is now abandoned and overgrown. There was a menagerie too in this part of the park, with birds from 'a thousand islands'.

Much planting occurred during these years and the group of cedars (**65**) south-east of the house by the lake was planted by Mrs Robert Child to commemorate the birth of her grandchild Sarah Sophia. It was this girl who married the 5th Earl of Jersey, whose family gave the property to the National Trust.

The main entrance to the Park is in Jersey Road, a turning off Thornbury Road on the Great West Road. Pasture spreads on either side of the southern avenue, which is bordered by massive Sweet Chestnuts. Horses and a pony welcome a friendly pat and any long grass you should care to offer; the little house opposite, towards the end of the avenue, sells fruit, eggs and vegetables; a herd of cows munches lazily in the field beyond.

At the end of the avenue, the southern lake comes into view, with the house (run by the Victoria and Albert Museum) slightly set back from it. Willows and alders fringe the lakeside, and here you will notice the old cedars, and a little way along a Cork Oak (*Quercus suber*), now surrounded by railings. To the north of the house stand the handsome red-brick Tudor stables, with an 18th-century clocktower. Refreshments are served here in summer. The walled vegetable garden at the back is now used for propagating plants, and next to it curves the elegant semicircular summer-house designed by Adam. This would have been used for storing plants, and its rounded shape ensures maximum sunlight for them. A few orange trees now receive the benefit of this careful planning. Adam also produced an orangery, destroyed in World War II. John James's small temple nearby is a summer-house of another kind and dates from around 1720.

In the western part of the park the grass is long and lush and many of the trees are uncommon. The woods around the lake near the house consist of old yews and many oaks, including several Hungarian Oaks (*Quercus frainetto*). These were planted perhaps as long as 146 years ago, which means they be may be the oldest in the country, as the species was only introduced to Britain in 1838. A Pignut Tree (*Carya glabra*), 77 inches in girth, can be found at the western corner of the house, and north of the temple are a Yellow Catalpa (*Catalpa ovata*) and one of the oldest Prince Albert Yews in England. Also spread about are Daimyo Oaks (*Quercus dentata*), at 45 feet high some of the highest in Britain. North-east of the house an avenue of Red Horse Chestnuts runs towards Jubilee Lodge, the last outpost before the M4 motorway. Turn right for the northernmost lake, where you can fish or merely sit and admire the birdlife.

66 *A Megalosaurus – one of the twenty-nine stone prehistoric animals made in 1852–3 for Crystal Palace park by Benjamin Waterhouse Hawkins, under the direction of the zoologist and palaeontologist Professor Richard Owen.*

The Rookery and Crystal Palace

On Streatham Common there once stood a house called The Rookery. Today, although the mansion is long gone, its gardens, south of Streatham Common North, are still open to the public. Mineral springs were discovered in Streatham at the start of the 18th century and the village instantly achieved fame. The medicinal waters rivalled those offered at Epsom: three glasses were considered equal to nine of Epsom salts. Visitors thronging to the spa could find accommodation at Rookery House. It was originally called Streatham Well or Well House because one of the springs lay within its boundaries (today the site is marked by a well). In 1826 a new owner, James Coster, renamed the mansion The Rookery. In 1911 the local authority and residents bought the 3-acre garden, which was made public two years later.

At the main gates you confront a lawn sloping to the south-east, planted with mature cedars. Three date from *c.* 1780 and are therefore among the oldest in England. A rock garden is found on the north side of the garden, complete with a pool, a gentle stream, tall ligularia plants, lilies, tritoma, rhododendrons, heathers and spring bulbs. Between the trees are distant views of Surrey hills. The former kitchen garden has become an old-fashioned English garden with

an ornamental pond, fountain, flagged walks and a rose pergola. Among the flowers in the wide beds you might see hollyhocks, sunflowers, delphiniums, Pot Marigolds and zinnias against a backing of Variegated Holly, yew and Golden Privet. Near the pond, with ferns visible beneath the paved surround, is the well, over which a canopied pump-house once stood. Contrasting with this blaze of colour is the lovely White Flower Garden beyond, laid out by one of the last owners for a family wedding celebration. It demonstrates the subtlety with which white blooms must be combined.

After Streatham, why not pay a quick visit to Crystal Palace? Joseph Paxton's glass hall was moved here from Hyde Park after the Great Exhibition of 1851 and remained until fire devastated it in 1936. Today the park houses another centre for mass gatherings, the National and Youth Sports Stadium, holding 12,000 spectators. Here too is a small children's zoo, but it is the artificial rather than the live animals which attract attention: Crystal Palace park is the setting for a weird and wonderful collection of model prehistoric beasts (**66**). The best gate by which to reach these is not the main one, but a side entrance by the railway bridge on Thicket Road. The twenty-nine Victorian monsters are of brick and iron covered in stucco, and wallow in the water of the lake, perch on the island and lurk among bushes on the shore. They were designed for the park by Benjamin Waterhouse Hawkins and include an Ichthyosaurus, a Mega-

OVERLEAF
67 *Autumn leaves beautify Syon Park's Long Lake, which owes its present form to Capability Brown's reshaping of the park between 1763 and 1773. He was responsible for the planting round the ¼-mile-long lake.*

99

losaurus and a Giant Sloth. On New Year's Eve 1853 a banquet for twenty-one men was held in the bottom half of the Iguanodon. Although later research has revealed that the models are not entirely accurate representations of these dinosaurs, they are a pleasant vestige of the Great Exhibition era, as is a Monkey Puzzle tree (*Araucaria araucana*), a favourite with the Victorians, near the Iguanodon.

Syon Park

Syon Park boasts not only a large Tudor house and decorative gardens but also a gardening centre, a butterfly collection, a motor museum, an aviary, an aquarium, an art centre, souvenir and wholefood shops, a café and a restaurant. You could easily spend the whole day here.

In 1431 the land belonged to Syon Monastery of the English Bridgettine order. Some walls and a barn in the grounds are the only remains. Henry VIII dissolved the monastery in 1539 and after that the house was the scene of two gloomy episodes. Katherine Howard, Henry's fifth wife, was incarcerated here for four months before being beheaded, and five years later, in 1547, Henry stopped off en route to his own interment at Windsor.

Following this the Protector, the Duke of Somerset, took the land and replaced the monastery with the Tudor dwelling seen today. He surrounded his estate with brick walls and established one of the first botanic gardens in England. Among the rarer species were Mulberry bushes, still grown on the north side of the house. But Somerset was not to enjoy the fruits of his labours for long, for he too was beheaded on a charge of treason.

At the beginning of the 17th century, Henry Percy, 9th Earl of Northumberland, secured a lease for the house, and his descendants occupy the premises today. Henry renovated the building, constructed the two white 'pepperpot' lodges on the west lawn and refurbished the stables. But this Earl, too, proved unlucky and was forced to leave his rooms at Syon for some at the Tower of London, after having been falsely implicated in the Gunpowder Plot. The 10th Earl added many exotic plants to the gardens and the Inigo Jones colonnade to the east front, but it was in the 1760s, with the 1st Duke of Northumberland, that both house and land took their present form. He employed the Adam brothers to transform the interior and Lancelot 'Capability' Brown to landscape the grounds. Many of the oaks, cedars, limes and beeches were Capability's saplings. Tudor formal gardens were supplanted by simple rolling lawns and groups of trees. Out went an artificial river; in came two lakes, one in the formal gardens and the other in the western parkland.

The main gates of the park are on Syon Park Road and so if you drive, cycle or walk, you will come up the long avenue which skirts green pasture grazed by sheep. Once you have parked in the free car park you may wish first to visit the house. Or you can double back along the wall to the Rose Garden, which has 400 species and varieties. South of the house the roses are planted in geometric beds on a terrace – mainly floribunda and standard types; shrubs are in the open glade, and climbers mount a pergola, together with clematis. Beyond the water meadows and on the other side of the Thames lie Kew Gardens (see pp. 59–69). Among the trees notice the Cedars of Lebanon and (near the wall by the entrance) an extremely rare *Quercus infectoria*. There are only five specimens in Britain and this one is 58 feet tall.

68 *A statue of Flora, goddess of flowers, stands on a pedestal overlooking Syon's lawns. She is surrounded by a fine collection of oak trees, including a Shingle Oak from America, a Hungarian Oak and a Swamp Oak.*

North of the building, beyond the garden centre, you find the formal garden. The south-west corner is dominated by the Great Conservatory (**69**), constructed from Bath stone and gun-metal with exquisite tracery and cast-iron pillars. Charles Fowler designed it in 1822–7 for the 3rd Duke and the result is said to have inspired Joseph Paxton's conservatory for the Duke of Devonshire at Chatsworth and, of course, the Great Exhibition hall. There is an aviary with a family of garishly coloured Rosella parakeets. Tropical plants swelter beneath the dome, and in an adjacent wing humming birds and tanagers fly among more exotic plants, such as the vine which commemorates a shipment of cuttings sent from Syon to Sidney in 1832 to help found the Australian wine industry.

In another area of the conservatory gold carp swim in a pool engulfed in ferns, while two glass-sided beehives show their inmates at work. Try to spot the Queen, picked out by a white dot on her back. The aquarium next door contains busts, frescoes, and tanks raised on ornate legs. Swimming nonchalantly are guppies, sinister Natterer's piranha, shubunkins, Kissing Gourami and Crucian Carp. Red-Eared Turtles live here too, as does an Iguana, which you only know is not a model because it winks at you.

South of the conservatory is the formal Conservatory Flower Garden with its small pool graced by a figure of Mercury and flanked by beds of lavender. Laid out around 1830, it has two gorgeous *Magnolia denudata* which flaunt their cream flowers in June. Growing here too is the only Afghan Ash (*Fraxinus xanthoxyloides*) of notable size in Britain. The rock garden displays its Alpine plants on stones shipped over from Greece more than a hundred years ago.

OVERLEAF
69 *The magnificent and elegant conservatory at Syon was designed by Charles Fowler for the 3rd Duke of Northumberland and built 1822–7. Made of gun-metal and Bath stone, with window tracery and interior supporting columns of cast iron, it is 382 feet long and 65 feet wide. The garden in front, with its small pond and statue of Mercury, was laid out c. 1830.*

North of the conservatory in the middle of the lawn rises a Pride of India tree (*Koelreuteria paniculata*), and here too look out for the pinky-grey bark of the rare Bamboo-Leafed Oak (*Quercus vibrayeana*). The beds along the edge of the lake are flooded with colour from South African Lilies (*Agapanthus*), fuchsias and azaleas, but are no match for the peacocks which amble freely in the park.

The best view of Capability's lake (**67**) is from the end. A million cubic feet of soil were shifted to make this ¼-mile-long stretch. Swamp Cypresses, willows, beech and oak crowd densely along the banks while Tiger Lilies, willowherb and irises edge the water, and in spring glorious drifts of daffodils dress the northern shore. The woodland garden is about a third of the way along the lake; it has the tallest *Liquidambar* in Britain (93 feet). Further along, on the left of the main path, pause to admire the Caucasian Elm (*Zelkova carpinifolia*), towering 100 feet high. Just beyond is Flora's Lawn, named after the goddess of flowers, whose statue is balanced on a Doric column (**68**). The present figure is fibreglass, a replica of the 19th-century original; her hairpin acts as a lightning conductor. Behind Flora are two fine oaks: the rare Swamp White Oak (*Quercus bicolor*), over 70 feet high, and a Hungarian Oak (*Quercus frainetto*), possibly planted in 1840 and thus one of the first in this country. The beds about Flora are devoted to herbaceous perennials: Red-Hot Pokers, Black-Eyed Susie, globe thistles, lilies and asters. When all around looks bleak and bare in winter, the heather beds to the east near the end of the lake dazzle the eye.

Waterlow Park

In November 1889 Sir Sidney Waterlow sent a letter to the first chairman of the London County Council. In it he described a property he owned in Highgate, praising its hilly wooded land and ornamental water fed by natural springs. Sir Sidney stated that he felt one of the best ways to help the deprived working classes would be to supply them not only with housing but also with fresh air in the form of parks and recreation areas. He finished the letter by expressing his desire to help in providing large 'gardens for the gardenless', and presented to the council as a free gift 'my entire interest in my estate'. Today the lucky Highgate residents can still enjoy Waterlow Park under the philanthropic gaze of their patron's statue.

Of course, Sir Sidney was not the first or only owner. The mansion, known as Lauderdale House, was built in 1660 as a home for the ambitious Duke of the same name (see also Ham House, p. 83). A second tenant was the actress Nell Gwyn, whose marble bath can be seen set in a wall inside the house, next to the restaurant. Nell was concerned that her illegitimate son by the King should be provided for. So one day when Charles II was approaching the house, she dangled the baby from the window, threatening to drop him unless his father did something for him. Charles tactfully replied 'Save the Earl of Burford.'

70 Catalpa bignonioides *(Indian Bean Tree) leaves in Syon Park.*

OVERLEAF
71 *Dahlias in Waterlow Park, which has a special reputation for its brilliantly coloured flower-beds and splendid trees.*

Walking down Highgate Hill to the park's main entrance, you pass a plaque on the wall stating that Andrew Marvell, the 17th-century poet and Parliamentarian, had a cottage here. It was demolished in 1869, leaving a single stone step. Directly behind elegant white Lauderdale House two raised flower-beds contain a scented garden for the blind, and nearby is a sundial said to be level with the dome of St Paul's Cathedral. Old 16th-century brick walls encircle the Lauderdale gardens, and at the extreme western end of the terrace you have a good view of the undulating land (excellent for winter tobogganing), boasting three lakes, all at different levels and with their own colonies of bird life.

Steps just behind the house lead south into a formal area. This in turn has a second set of steps at its western end, which is flanked by eagles, bearers of the Lauderdale arms but left headless by the passing of time. The aviary, south of this formal garden, has Asian and South American birds in a much better state of health. Here too are shrubberies and herbaceous beds which glow with summer colour (**71**); in winter Christmas Roses take over. North of the house

stands the statue of Sir Sidney Waterlow in a setting of such English trees as oak, yew, lime and beech.

Wandering by the south-west boundary you will notice on the other side of the railings some of the 51,000 graves of the famous Highgate Cemetery. In this modern section lie Karl Marx, picked out by his monstrous effigy (**72**), George Eliot and Sir Ralph Richardson. But the old part is more interesting, on the other side of Swains Lane, at the bottom of the park. It was opened in 1839 and the arrangement of the tombs is highly stylised, in the form of, for example, an Egyptian avenue, Lebanon circle and terraced catacombs. Mourning Victorian angels appear tangled in creepers and surrounded by wild flowers. Today you must take a guided tour to see just a small area and you may stumble on the graves of such men and women as Christina Rossetti, Radclyffe Hall, and the parents of Charles Dickens.

72 *Highgate Cemetery was opened in 1839 as an alternative to the overcrowded metropolitan cemeteries. It soon became full itself; this view, from Waterlow Park, is of the extension, opened in 1854. In the distance is the vast bust which surmounts the grave of Karl Marx (d. 1883). Guided tours are provided of the major monuments in the old part, many of them hard to find in the undergrowth.*

Seasonal Guide

Month	Plants in Season and Areas of Special Interest
January–February	Christmas Rose, Winter Jasmine, Winter Honeysuckle, Witch Hazel, snowdrops, Mimosa
	Heather gardens: Kew; Isabella Plantation and Pembroke Lodge, Richmond; Cannizaro; Syon Alpine House: Kew Australian House: Kew
March–April	Crocus, magnolia, flowering almond, Forsythia, grape hyacinth, polyanthus, Wallflower
	Spring bedding: sunken garden and Flower Walk, Kensington; Hampton Court; Cannizaro; Holland Park; Gunnersbury; Chelsea Hospital; St James's; Broad Walk, Kew; Greenwich; Chiswick; Hyde Park Woodland Garden: Syon Bluebells: Queen Charlotte's Cottage grounds, Kew Rock Garden: Kew Wild peonies: Chelsea Physic Garden Wild flowers: Orleans House; Kenwood
May–June	Clematis, tulip, peony, pansy, hyacinth, forget-me-not, foxglove, lilac, wisteria, lupin, delphinium, periwinkle, stock, Sweet William, viburnum
	Laburnum: Queen's Garden, Kew; Hampton Court Iris Garden: Kew; Holland Park Azaleas: Isabella Plantation, Richmond; Waterhouse Woodland Garden, Bushy Park; Cannizaro; The Hill; Kew Camellias: Syon; Chiswick Alpine Rock Garden: Kew Tropical Waterlily House: Kew Horse Chestnuts: Bushy Park; Cannizaro Formal bedding and herbaceous borders: sunken garden and Flower Walk, Kensington; Kew; St John's Lodge, Broad Walk and Queen Mary's Garden, Regent's Park; Hampton Court; Greenwich; The Rookery; Golders Hill; Gunnersbury; Cannizaro; Holland Park; Tradescant; Syon; Chiswick; York House; Waterlow Rhododendrons: Richmond; Cannizaro; Waterlow; The Hill; Kenwood Roses: Ham; Syon; Kew; St James's; Queen Mary's Garden, Regent's Park; Greenwich; Hampton Court; York House Magnolia: Great Conservatory Garden, Syon

July–August	Begonia, pinks, fuchsia, lobelia, geranium, lavender, petunia, marigold, salvia, zinnia, Red-Hot Poker, clematis, Hollyhock, phlox, sunflower, Morning Glory, Sweet Pea

Great Vine: Hampton Court
Pomegranate: Tradescant; Cannizaro; Kew; Chelsea Physic Garden

September–October	Aster, dahlia, hebe, hydrangea, Michaelmas Daisy

Heather gardens: Kew; Syon; Pembroke Lodge, Richmond
Bracken: Richmond
Autumnal trees: Kensington; Richmond; Osterley; Hampstead Heath; Holland Park; Syon; Kenwood; Regent's Park; Primrose Hill; Chiswick; Marble Hill; Orleans House; Crystal Palace; Hyde Park
Woodland area: Chelsea Physic Garden

November–December	Winter-Flowering Cherry, *Viburnum fragrans*, Witch Hazel, holly, cotoneaster

Alpine House: Kew

73 *Would-be collectors pause to examine paintings hung by their artists along the Bayswater Road, on the railings of Hyde Park.*